Praise for *If Through It, We Do It:*

This book should be in every high school library as required reading. Joey's proved that every American has the opportunity to become a successful owner of his/her business, without a college degree, and be part of the American Dream.

Joey is the ultimate entrepreneur and a blue-collar worker who built an incredibly dynamic business by being a visionary and by applying dedication, perseverance, and just plain hard work.

My wife Katherine and I were fortunate to have had a plumbing problem 35 years ago and to have found a lifetime friend.

—Tom Anderson, diplomat and US Ambassador from 1984 to 1986 under President Ronald W. Reagan

Joey's book should be read by every young boy or girl finishing high school who is thinking about their life and career, and most of all, their passion. They could learn from his six core values and the many quotes throughout his book. One of my favorites was from his father: "avoiding wasted motion." Joey's final tribute to the Town of Middleburg filled my eyes with tears. The book is a wonderful read.

—Catherine "Bundles" Murdock, recipient of the State Department's Distinguished Honor Award, local luminary, and Middleburg Town Council member for 12 years

Joey Snider's *If Water Runs Through It, We Do It!* is an incredible guidebook for aspiring plumbers and master plumbers alike. But wait, it's more than just a guidebook for plumbers, as Joey personalizes his journey to becoming the founder of one of the most trusted plumbing services in Virginia. You will learn about the hills and valleys that can be expected as you start in the profession, the gotcha moments that will happen as you rise in stature, and then the benefits of building trust with employees and the community. All of which are offset by the colorful anecdotes that make this a great read for anyone. Many of the lessons learned in *If Water Runs Through It, We Do It!* convey the everyday challenges of life. No matter what you do for a living, this book offers insight that you will find relevant. It's a must-read.

—A.J. Panebianco, Retired Chief of Police, 2021–2022 President of the Virginia Chiefs of Police Association & Foundation

If Water Runs Through It, We Do It! is a quick and enjoyable read by Joey Snider.

Snider Plumbing is an iconic business in our area. Ray Snider was our plumber in the '90s. Three decades later, Joey and his team became our new best friends. We had constant issues at our farm—frozen pipes, frozen horse watering systems, busted pipes and backed-up toilets—but J.R. Snider and his team always responded quickly to take care of our problems. The folks at J.R. Snider are not only our plumbers, they are our neighbors. Enjoy what you do, and success will follow.

Those in the trades like plumbers, electricians, HVAC, stone masons, and carpenters are just as important as *any* white-collar job.

—Dea and Beau Van Metre, principals at Van Metre companies

I have known Joey Snider for many years and found him to be a hardworking, smart, entrepreneurial businessman. These traits shine in his collection of memories from his journey through the plumbing profession. The blend of personal humor and insights into the evolving role of service plumbers and business owners highlights the complexity of their work. He tells what it takes to be both.

This book is full of compelling reasons why today's service plumber is no longer just a blue-collar worker. It demonstrates the need for today's service plumber to be every bit as involved in today's various technologies as those professions requiring college degrees. An intriguing message about how the plumbing profession is multifaceted and requires continuous learning and adaptation.

Those interested in the plumbing industry or evaluating their life's path will do well to read this book.

—Larry G. Fanella, President May Supply Company, retired

Joey has put together a book that should be read by everyone, but especially by those in their junior year of high school. I have seen firsthand how his young apprentices matured into great plumbers within a short period. Do yourself a favor and get your sons and daughters to read this book. It's a great read and also an investment in their future.

—Bob Ball, proprietor of a hardware and lumber supply store, and community builder in Middleburg

I have been a client of Joey Snider Plumbing for over 30 years. Joey's superior level of service can only be achieved by hands-on training. Joey's staff embraced his vision of knowledge and customer service. Speaking as someone who has been in business for 40+ years, if you don't instill the vision in your team, then it's simply a race to the bottom. Joey Snider is the consummate business leader.

—Bill Jackson, Founder/President Tri-County Feeds, Fashions, Finds

If Water Runs Through It, We Do It! was an easy read and very interesting to me as I spent many years in the plumbing supply industry. I often wondered what type of service plumber I would have been and if I would have been successful. I wish my boss would have been more like Joey. This would be a good book for high school kids to read.

—Kenneth May, shareholder of May Supply, an inventory supply company, retired

A book that is very well done. Once you think you have learned everything about your trade, you're about halfway there. The business end is much more difficult.

—Dennis Singhas, President of Valley Drilling Corp. of VA

Fantastic book! A must-read for any entrepreneur looking to go from getting the work done to working on a successful business. It's all about the people you choose to be around! Congratulations on such a successful career, business, life, and now a great book! I am so proud of you! I always said we need to strive to be as good as J.R. Snider so we can charge the prices we need to get.

—Mike Appleton, president of Appleton Campbell (plumbing, heating, air conditioning, electrical service company), friend and competitor

Get ready to be inspired and gain invaluable insights into the world of service plumbing! This book is a must-read for anyone considering a career in the trades. Through real-life experiences from a service plumbing business owner, you'll discover the challenges, triumphs, and wisdom that come with this rewarding profession. Whether you're considering a career in the trades, just starting out, or looking to grow your own business, this book offers practical advice and heartfelt encouragement that will fuel your passion and set you up for success.

The journey of Joey Snider and his team, known as "Snider's Riders," is a testament to the hard work, dedication, and passion required to succeed in this field. Through their experiences, aspiring tradespeople will gain a deep understanding of what it takes to thrive in the trades.

Joey's leadership and the camaraderie of Snider's Riders shine through, making this book not just informative but also incredibly inspiring. This book is your road map to a fulfilling and successful future in the trades!

—Dennis A. Taylor, co-owner of Paradigm Solutions, business coach, mentor, consultant, facilitator

A great read—old-fashioned determination and work ethic meet modern forward thinking. A success story humbly delivered with humor. Our town, friends, and customers benefited from your company's legacy. A fun, easy read that provides great real-life advice. May be more useful than an MBA!

—Helen MacMahon, family friend and real estate broker

Life is a learning curve, and my friend Joey Snider captures this perfectly in an entertaining way in his book. I have always been passionate about training horses and he about plumbing. Follow your passion and good things will come.

—Kim Keppick, a trainer who puts horses and people together properly. A specialist in all equestrian disciplines

I'm a self-employed bookkeeper in the Middleburg area and have known Joey since 2014. He was then on the board of a local nonprofit, and we met when I was asked to take them on as a client. I quickly learned that with Joey, there is no pretense. He's honest, has a kind and empathetic heart, and a great mind for business.

Several years later he asked me to take over the bookkeeping at J.R. Snider. I took it over on a "temporary" basis. Today, he's still a client. The better I got to know him and his wife Kristi, the more impressed I was with his commitment to his family, his business, his employees, and his community. It doesn't surprise me in the least that he would end up writing a book with the goal of educating young people and promoting entrepreneurship. He regularly met with his employees individually and as a group to try to help them understand how to manage their funds and their futures. Some listened and some didn't, but he never gave up.

Joey was always looking for ways to improve not only his bottom line but his business and his customer service. He absolutely succeeded in both. This book has a lot to offer, but like his employees, you need to be willing to listen and learn. It's a book to save and use as a reference again and again.

—Mary Deppa, CFO of JR Snider Ltd.

I had the privilege of working closely with Joey Snider during the final stages of his impressive entrepreneurial journey. As his business coach, I witnessed firsthand the dedication and drive that defined Joey's approach to business. His book, *If Water Runs Through It, We Do It!*, encapsulates his wealth of knowledge and passion for building a successful business.

Joey shares his humorous short stories and practical lessons in a friendly way, giving us a glimpse into the plumbing industry. His personal experiences offer valuable lessons relevant to plumbers and other small-business owners. He stresses the importance of building a business based on a passion for what you do and creating and implementing shared values as keys to success.

Reading his book brings back memories of our many conversations during our coaching relationship. Joey's sincerity comes through, and his passion is evident. This book is a must-read for anyone seeking wisdom, humor, and a fresh perspective on business. Joey Snider's journey inspires us all.

—Marty Paradise, Paradise Business Coaching

Well done and to the point. It's a mini version of the American way.

—Paul MacMahon, family friend and real estate broker

A must-read and reference for anyone starting a business. The lessons apply to any type of business.

I was a customer of Joey's for 35 years, and I can tell you he understood that customer service is what kept his business growing. Here is one example of that. One cold February morning, I woke up to the sound of running water at 3 a.m. A pipe had burst, and I had to get the water shut off, but not before filling up the coffee pot. I knew I had a fair amount of damage, so my first call was to Snider. Expecting to get an answering machine, imagine my surprise when a person answered. I explained what happened, and after a short "hold on," Joey himself was on the line. He told me he was on his way until I explained he could send a crew in the morning. This made me feel very special, and I know that's how he made all his customers feel.

—Carolyn Saffer, former client, friend, and colleague

Joey Snider and his father, Ray Snider, were the best plumbers in the area and two of the finest men who have contributed so much to this community. *If Water Runs Through It, We Do It!* is quite entertaining. This book contains amazing short stories and inspiring life lessons that everyone will enjoy reading.

—Mildred Fletcher Slater, personal friend, confidante, and one hell of an Attorney

Joey's book should be required reading for anyone considering owning any type of service business. He clearly identifies the danger of not knowing exactly what it costs to provide every service on offer. He is absolutely correct that many owners would be better off financially and emotionally working for someone else.

Parents and students should heed his comments on university vs. a journeyman path in the trades. This is a discussion that we've needed for a long time. We have lots of educated paupers who can recite poetry, but few folks who can earn a living by fixing things.

—Helen Modly, former wealth manager and advisory team leader at Buckingham Strategic Wealth, now retired

IF WATER RUNS THROUGH IT, WE DO IT!

Adventures of a Service Plumber from
Apprentice to Seven-Figure Business Owner

JOEY SNIDER

Printed and bound in the United States of America
ISBN: 979-8-218-36365-9

Back cover photo: Joey and Kristi Snider with two of our beloved
dogs, Franklin T. Copperfield (left) and Daisy Duke (right).

DEDICATION

To my mom for her hard and endless work raising
five children and making sure we all received a good
education in both school and social life.
To my dad for his tireless dedication to his family
while creating the foundation for my career.

CONTENTS

PREFACE

Four months after I retired in April of 2023, I found myself on my farm situated at the top of a small mountain. It was 5:00 AM and as I sat in my blind, I was listening to spring gobblers sounding off on their roosts. I've always enjoyed imitating the yelp of a mature hen (female turkey) to entice the gobbler (male turkey) to come close enough to videotape.

I was drinking coffee from my thermos and enjoying the fresh mountain air when inspiration hit me!

I pulled out my phone and sent myself an email that outlined several chapters and what they would relate to. Over the next five weeks of spring gobbler season, I would get to the top of the mountain between 4:30 and 5:00 AM, drink my coffee, listen to the barred owls, and wait for the gobblers to start their morning rituals as I imitated a lonely and lovesick hen at daybreak. As I sat there, my mind went back in time and retrieved the stories and events that I had stored in my brain. I wrote as fast as I could think.

After a few weeks, I began organizing the material into chapters, and the next thing I knew, I was actually writing a book! A few more weeks and voila, my business memoir was complete.

Over the years I spent as both a service plumber and a business owner I faced some trying times, some funny times, and some things you experience that make you say to yourself, "You can't make this stuff up!"

I used to jokingly say, "I'll put that in my book when I retire!"

I have had the rare opportunity to have a job that created both pleasure and a good living. I want to share some of it with you to shed light on the experience of being a service plumber. Although I was a service plumber, the actual lessons learned apply to anyone in the service industry. The types of businesses and the services we offer may differ, but many of the challenges we encounter are very much the same.

In this book I share my journey, short stories, and some of my personal life and beliefs. I hope it makes the reader smile, laugh, and perhaps makes life better by learning from some relatable mistakes!

I had a friend ask me why I would take the time to write a book, and who's going to read it. Initially, I didn't have much of a reason for sharing my thoughts, trials, lessons learned, and experience. I almost convinced myself it was merely an ego boost after retirement.

Then I was reminded by that little voice we all have: "You owe it to those coming up behind you. Share the knowledge you gained from those who went before you."

That is why I'm writing this book. I hope that I attract the audience of those at a crossroads in their life and also those that may have influence over young people who are deciding how to make a living doing something they enjoy.

Over the course of my life, I've observed people who are successful financially, and have tried to emulate them. I have seen the difference between wealthy people and happy people and then those few who are both. It is my opinion that those who have both financial and personal happiness generally love what they do for a living. They have followed their passion.

I'm writing this book to convey my passion for the trades. I love plumbing, drain cleaning, gas pipe work, and grew to be fascinated with water treatment. It's an industry that the world needs forever.

I hope that my short stories, my opinions, and my advice is interesting and inspirational to both young men and women that are curious about the trades. If this book helps one person find a hidden passion, then I will be very happy and proud and consider my time well spent.

PART ONE

A PLUMBING LEGACY

A BRIEF HISTORY OF MY PLUMBING CAREER

I suppose it's only fitting to start with my father, Ray Snider, who in 1967 at the age of 36 decided to leave a prestigious job as plumbing superintendent for high-rises in Washington, D.C., and start a small plumbing company, 60 miles west of Washington, D.C., in a small town called The Plains.

So it began. I was nine years old, one of 5 children.

I idolized my father. I was always in his back pocket. By the age of 10 I was riding along with him most days during summer break and holidays. When my father worked in the city, he left at 4:30 AM, so I didn't see much of him. But now he was all mine. I'm not sure how he made me feel so important, but somehow, he did. If I overslept, he was gone, and I missed a day's work. I felt bad that he didn't have any help, so I learned very early to be an early riser.

By the age of 12 I finally became useful, and by 13 I could make my first solder joint. My father was a patient man. He told me to be quiet and learn by watching when we were inside a customer's home.

By 15 years of age, I could handily use two pipe wrenches and was prepping unions, male adapters and relief valves for water heater replacements. I remember asking my father, "How do you know when a fitting on a pipe is tight enough so it wouldn't leak?" He said, "Tight is tight, too tight is as bad as too loose." I said okay and left it at that.

By age 16 I learned to drive his service truck, which was an old "Charles Chips" van with a 4-speed transmission. Back in the day, potato chips were delivered to your doorstep. Dad's brother rebuilt the engine, and that truck ran for years.

By age 17, still in high school, I was an apprentice and put on larger jobs on summer break to prove myself.

My dad tried to run me out of the trade by putting me in charge of cutting and threading steel and galvanized pipe for two plumbers on new construction jobs. One plumber was running steel gas lines and the other drains, waste lines and vents. This went on for 9 hours a day, 5 days a week, and then I helped him on weekends with well pumps and water heater replacements—oh, and sewer stoppages too. My dad tried to discourage me from doing what he did because he wanted me to have a better life and living than he had.

At 18 years of age, my mother and father confronted me with college. I had always wanted to be a Forest Ranger and now I was at a crossroads. I had been accepted at Virginia Polytechnic Institute (which became Virginia Tech) but decided to go to community college first and continue my plumbing apprenticeship while not in school.

Well, my college schedule, as my dad said, was "not applicable" for the job he had to offer. My mother wouldn't allow me to quit school, so I was terminated from the plumbing company for the time being. I got a job with a local cabinetmaker that allowed me to work around my college classes.

At 20 years of age I graduated from community college, had my associate degree, and discussed my future in plumbing with my parents. They agreed that my passion for the trade was more than my prior dreams of becoming a Forest Ranger. My dad said he'd hire me back if I signed up for a state apprenticeship program and had my master plumbing and gas licensing in two years. At this time, you had to have 5 years of experience under a master plumber, of which two were in a supervisory role. Thus, the two-year deadline my father stated.

At age 22 I was a master plumber and gas fitter. Three years later my father called me into his office. I thought I was getting a raise and promotion as I had just finished up a huge project. To my dismay, the conversation was about his being ready to slow down. It was time for me to either buy his company or get another job. Holy moly, I wasn't ready for that! But I put my resume out in the market and found another job.

The job I signed up for was strictly new construction, and I already knew my true passion was the service side of plumbing. I sat down with my parents and asked how in the hell I would pay for the company if I decided to change my mind.

August 1st, 1983, it was official. I talked my younger brother into going in with me, so we named the new company Snider Bros. Plumbing Co.

PAY PHONES, TWO-WAY RADIOS, AND PAGERS— OH MY!

My journey through technology has been both evolutionary and revolutionary!

As time changes all things, so it was with how I adapted to new technology. In the early '80s we had to find a pay phone to call our answering machine that our customers left messages on. We called our shop, and upon hearing the recording pushed the "star" button, put in our password and boom—we could retrieve our messages!! For another 50 cents we could return a few calls and keep in touch with our clients.

Well, then we got pagers (yes, we wore them proudly on our belt). First, the numeric pager that told you the number of who was calling! It was very exciting and cutting edge to say the least. Customers could even punch in a code to alert us to an emergency!

Now it's the mid-1980s, and the company we got our pagers from upgraded their tower to provide "voice pagers" so our customers could leave us a 20-second message—a second device we wore proudly on our belt. So, you can picture us with a 12-foot Stanley tape measure and two pagers on our belt.

The mid-1980s were bursting with technological advancements! Next, we had two-way radios in all the trucks and two base stations, one at my home and one for regular hours at the shop. If dispatch needed to talk to a technician, you just sent them a note on their pager, and they could go to their truck and respond back on the two-way radio. We and one other company in our area were killing it with the level of customer service we could offer.

Then came the late 1980s and ushered in the "bag phone." I got several of them. No more pay phones for us, and yes, I did drive through Main Street with the phone to my ear so everyone could see that I had a portable phone!

We then went to phones that were mounted under the seat and the keypad and handheld piece of the phone was mounted on the dashboard right beside the two-way radio microphone. This was the envy of all the tradesmen when you pulled into a job site and accidentally left your door open!

We are wearing two styles of pagers, both numeric and voice, cell phones, and two-way radios. From the mid-'80s through the early '90s, we were the "cat's meow" of logistics in our service area. Our competitors were envious.

Then, in early 1993 came Nextel. That leveled the playing field overnight. This small device was a cell phone and a two-way radio built into one portable flip phone. Prior to this, within our 30-mile service area, there were only two companies using pagers and two-way radios. Overnight, the Nextel flip phone operated as a pager, a two-way radio and phone *and* they were affordable. Within a month, we were basically the same as everyone else. We did not want to become a dinosaur overnight, so, we replaced all of our pagers, phones, and two-way radios with this thing called Nextel. This is when I realized that it was worth the cost of staying on the cutting edge of technology.

The next step was GPS tracking in the trucks. I think it was around 1996 we did a trial run with this system. The salesman assured me the ROI would more than justify the up-front expenses. GPS allowed one person to see where all the technicians were simultaneously.

This technology was not exactly "real-time" at first but developed quickly into an accurate tool to allow a single dispatcher to become a logistical manager. So instead of offering what was usually a wait time of two or three days, we started offering "next-day services" with a 3-hour service window for many types of jobs! This put the heat back on our competition, and "Snider's Riders" were once again on top of our game!

Next was the internal GPS devices the technicians used instead of the large and unwieldy ADC map books. This was mind-blowing and a huge time saver, especially in city traffic. Productivity increased by approximately seven billable hours per week, per technician, with the use of GPS tracking for dispatch and another three hours per week, per tech, with internal GPS for directions to job addresses. That's 10 more productive hours per week per tech!

By now it's early to mid-2000s, and everyone has both types of GPS. What's next? It can't get any better, can it? We bought several laptop computers and attached printers to them. We could provide professionally written estimates the same day we assessed the jobs and left with a signed contract. We installed boilerplate pricing in a PDF for 50% of our standard tasks. Thus, the start of up-front pricing and no more time-and-materials mailed invoices. Only a couple of people in the company were able to operate these laptops at this point.

By 2006 we were completely (90%) up front, or as it was now called, "flat-rate pricing." Everything ran on a new software platform that was developed for a company that serviced elevators in office buildings. We were the guinea pig for this company that was located in the Midwest as they tested branching out into other trades.

So, now we are driven by GPS, price controlled by a price book, customer history, accounts receivable, accounts payable, and payroll all on the same software package. We are on autopilot! Well, things are moving faster technologically than we are learning. The old saying "garbage in, garbage out" comes to mind.

After some internal training and software updates, we are back on track and in late 2006 we are all using laptops, swiping credit cards on location, and billing and collecting upon completion of our services as long as cellular service was available.

By 2007 we were a well-oiled machine. Then 2008 came. Most of us remember the Great Recession.

We were in survival mode until mid-2011. Our technical advances and expenditures were put on hold.

When 2012 arrived, we are still cautious, but it's time to get back up on the horse and charge ahead. This year brought about a new way to reach our audience called Pay-Per-Click advertising. It had been around before but wasn't affordable to a small company. So, I hired a marketing management company. Then another. Fired them, then hired another. We are doing okay, but another lesson learned. If you're not the lead dog, the view never changes.

After a lot of pestering and many lunches, I finally got "vetted" by a major water treatment manufacturer in the USA. My company was now a dealer and had our own territory in which to do business. This dealership was a huge step in gaining traction in the new marketplace that is driven by the Internet, social media, and reviews. With this new partnership came resources of the likes a small company couldn't imagine.

By now it's 2016. We have a solid understanding of our new foundation. Our water treatment equipment is among the first to be Wi-Fi compatible, and the economy is positioned to explode.

We have accurate dashboards, an actual marketing budget with a purpose, and realistic goals to which we can be held accountable. Another lesson learned—If you can't measure it, you can't manage it. We headed into 2017 with a head of steam.

The year 2019 finds me in a dilemma. We've outgrown our facility that has been our comfort zone for many years. The technological advancements we received from our partnership with our water treatment manufacturing company have increased sales in all three divisions of the company. Lesson learned here is to not be run over by your own snowball.

By 2020, we've moved to a much larger facility. Exciting times for everyone as we can spread our wings and see the potential for further growth.

Not so much time between evaluations now. We are truly players in our marketplace. My job as President has changed, as I'm almost entirely the "vision" guy and not as much a part of the actual operations. Lesson learned, careful what you wish for.

Now it's 2021 and my financial leadership team tells me we need 12% to 15% growth in the next year.

The economy is strong, we have the correct strategies and certainly the technology to make it happen.

So we did.

It's mid-2022 and again I sit in front of my team, which consists of two coaches, my attorney, and my CFO.

The celebration is short-lived. Now the conversation is geared around something called the next "platform," which is the next financial level the company is heading into. Lesson learned, technology can make you or break you.

At the beginning of this chapter, there was a year or two between changes and advancements. Now, big changes are getting closer and closer together. Now it's months and at times weeks between when you have to be ready to change or to pull the trigger on either new technology, systems or methods. If you don't change and adapt, you'll get left behind.

Moving forward a couple of months to the third quarter of 2022 and I realize what was really going on. We had successfully conquered platform number 1 (between $800k– $1.5 million in revenue) with pure will and determination. Then, with the use of all we learned in the first platform, plus the proper use of technology, we arrived at the very top of platform number 3 ($2.5–$4 million in revenue).

Now it's the second week of the fourth quarter. Same leadership team as before. The topic is platform number 4 ($4–$6 million in revenue) and creating a roadmap to get there. This strategic map was a straight vertical line. No curves or crossroads to buy time or ponder. I was faced with two clear choices. Either invest in another layer of internal management to prepare ahead of time for the necessary growth or sell the company to someone who already had our core values and these Standard Operating Procedures (SOPs) in place.

The lesson learned here is that the hardest decision to make is one that doesn't have to be made right now.

Ten weeks later we are at the settlement table with a company that had pursued an acquisition of my company eighteen months earlier. Our company will prosper and flourish because of the acquisition. I'm proud to have been a part of the journey and I am looking forward to watching how the new leader uses technology to keep this company on the leading edge of the service industry.

In conclusion, while I enjoyed every challenge that technology offers, it's evident by my timelines that things are developing and changing at a much faster pace. I will never forget that my main goal was customer service, and all my decisions were based on keeping the company healthy in order to provide the best customer experience possible. I hope that moving forward so quickly doesn't allow technology to interfere with this vision.

PART TWO

WHAT DOES IT TAKE TO BE IN THE TRADES?

DIFFERENT TYPES OF PLUMBERS

There are basically three types of plumbers. They are Commercial, Residential, and Service Plumbers. My father was all three. That's very uncommon. I had the luxury of learning from him and gained a lot of experience at a young age.

In order to be an excellent service plumber you have to have prior experience in at least commercial or residential new construction for obvious reasons. There are pros and cons related to new construction plumbers and service plumbers.

If you are in new construction, you know where you are working, what time you start, what you will be doing, and what time your workday is done. If you decide to be a service plumber, disregard all the above and that's your job description. Being a service plumber is not for the majority of those in the trade. For me, it was how I was raised. I learned early that the "juice was definitely worth the squeeze." Plus, I've always enjoyed the instant gratification of helping people out of a situation that requires my expertise to solve a problem and make their lives better that same day.

OLD-TIMERS VERSUS TODAY'S PLUMBERS

'm writing this chapter from the standpoint of my dad, who would be 91 years old if he was still with us. Then I'll write what it was like to work for him as well as what the current workforce has to say about working for me. So, this chapter is basically my opinion on how the last three generations of tradesmen have evolved.

We will start with my dad in the year 1948. He joined the Navy before being drafted. He played the clarinet very well and was put into the Navy Band. He intentionally failed the tryouts so he could be a Seabee (the construction battalion for the Navy). His four years of military service during the Korean War were spent in the Construction Battalion. He came home and went to work for his uncle.

His uncle retired, and my father, living in Washington, D.C., applied for a commercial plumbing job in Virginia. He started as part of a crew. In a couple of years he's foreman, and five years later at age 27, he's superintendent in charge of 20 to 40 plumbers and gas fitters, fire suppression, as well as sewer and water crews.

His workweek was Monday through Friday. Saturdays were normally off unless weather delays had interfered with the schedule and concrete was being poured. Completely off on Sunday. Benefits package included a company station wagon for back and forth to work within 25 miles. Gasoline was provided for travel to work. One week of paid vacation. Time off for vacation was approved as long as jobs were on schedule and your duties were covered by approved personnel. There were no paid sick or personal days. There were six paid holidays: New Year's Day, Memorial Day, Independence Day, Labor Day, Thanksgiving Day, and Christmas Day.

Hours of operation were 6:30 AM until 4:00 PM. Thirty minutes unpaid for lunch. Two 15-minute paid breaks at 10:00 AM and 2:00 PM. If you were more than 10 minutes late to work, you were docked a half hour of pay for that day. If you missed more than one day per month, you were required to work late Monday through Friday to make up the time.

An hourly rate increase was between 25 to 50 cents per hour. The pay rate for a commercial plumber in 1958 was around $5,100 per year. No retirement or pensions available or offered at most non-union jobs during this time. Basically, you worked 2,200 hours per year, and you got paid for the time you worked. You provided your own hand tools, health insurance, and transportation.

Now it's 1967, my dad is 36 years old, and we've moved 60 miles west of his normal work area. Dad has decided to leave his cushy job and start his own residential plumbing company.

Moving forward to 1970, Dad was charging $8.50 per hour for his services. No travel time and an approximately 10% markup on materials.

By 1975 I was, at times, in my own truck on weekends and the rate was $14.50 per hour for one man and $17.25 for me and a helper. I was still part-time but making $4 per hour. Overtime was not a thing.

By 1980 Dad's hourly rate was $27.75 for a plumber and helper. I was making $7.50 per hour.

1983 is when my father decided to sell me and my brother the company. I was making $10 per hour and a plumber and helper went for $24.75 per hour. Our materials markup had risen to 15%.

I will now move on to the 2020s and what a service plumber's job description looks like. I had the luxury of a 3-year apprenticeship before being thrown to the wolves. With the lack of apprenticeship programs and the shortage of interest in the trades, today's tradesmen are not as well versed in all aspects of their chosen vocation. Many are "specialists" in certain portions of their trade and lack knowledge of other areas in their field. This is a cause and effect due to rising labor costs, which in turn made it cost- prohibitive to send a plumber's helper along most of the time. So, the apprentice position has been all but eliminated. Add in the illusion that blue-collar jobs are for uneducated people, and there you have it. Very few people are entering a career in the trades.

So, let's describe the ones that do go against the grain and dive into the position of a Service Plumber.

It takes a lot of confidence, as the apprenticeship is condensed into as little as six months to maybe a year.

The emphasis in many cases is about productivity rather than quality of workmanship and customer service. It's a type of pressure that I didn't endure. Today's service plumbers must find a company that has properly aligned core values as well as a training program in place to keep up with changing technology.

Today plumbers are referred to as level 1, 2, and 3:

A level 1 service plumber usually has six months to one year of experience and can complete minor plumbing repairs and replacements. Average pay rate is $17 to $19 per hour. They get a week's paid vacation, six paid holidays and 50% employer-paid health insurance.

A level 2 service plumber usually has one to three years of experience. They can complete 80% of plumbing repairs and replacements. They are still in need of support and minor supervision. Average pay rate is $20 to $25 per hour. They get one-week paid vacation, six paid holidays, 50% employer-paid health insurance, company vehicle, gas card and tool allowance. All hours worked past eight hours in a workday are at time-and-a-half rate.

A level 3 service plumber usually has three to five years of experience. They are able to complete most plumbing tasks without supervision. Their diagnostic skill set is almost that of a supervisor. They have excellent communication skills as well as an ability to present solutions on a "good, better, best" platform to clients.

Average pay rate for this position is better described in terms of yearly income from $60,000 up to $180,000, and much more in some markets. Once you get to this point (3 to 5 years, which seems like a lot of time in the minds of today's workforce), it's really up to the individual.

How much skin do you want to put in the game? You've proven that you can work independently for the most part. Obviously, you have conquered the vertical learning curve. You don't have student loans to pay off, and you have very little competition in the workplace. At this point you probably have 2 or 3 weeks of PTO, 6 paid holidays, 3% to 6% 401k company match, 50% employer-paid health insur-

ance, short- and long-term disability insurance benefits, company vehicle, gas card, tool allowance, profit
sharing or SPIFF program eligibility. First in line for
high-level training with travel and payroll expenses
covered. The benefit packages for this level of individual are incredible and becoming more lucrative
every year.

To sum it up, today's service plumber still needs
all the attributes of the old-timers. Yes, things aren't
quite as heavy and painstakingly involved to install
and repair. But that's traded for the constant need for
further and continuing education to keep up with
today's fast-paced world.

INTESTINAL FORTITUDE

What does it take to truly be a professional plumbing service provider? There are many opinions
on this topic, but here's my theory. It all comes down
to intestinal fortitude. Those two words contain the
magic bullet of success.

These two words, used together, are very powerful
in my opinion. Fortitude means courage. But used

after the word intestinal, you now have a human characteristic or trait that comes from the gut. Now we mix courage with determination, and that, my friends, is one of the most important pieces of being a professional service plumber, and just a good human being for that matter.

The ingredients of "intestinal fortitude" are as follows:

Passion, dedication, intelligence, willingness, discipline, fearlessness, respectfulness. If you notice, there is no mention of pipe wrenches, fancy lettered trucks, or high-tech tools. That's because they are all useless without intestinal fortitude.

I believe this trait is not something you are just born with—it's a learned behavior. So those that have been blessed by this type of circle of influence have an obligation to pass it on to someone else and keep our future generations healthy and strong.

You can be the smartest person in the entire company, but you will always come in second to the person that has intestinal fortitude. This trait is often found in people that are punctual, consistent, resilient, empowered, and aware of their surroundings. I've always tried to emulate people with this trait. My father had it. I've worked hard to surround myself with people who have it. I refer to Stephen Covey's circle of influence and try to stay in an area I can control. You can control who you work for and with.

Now that we have the ingredients of a service plumber, let's put them together and describe this person and the value they will bring to the job market.

THE DNA OF "SNIDER'S RIDERS"

There is a saying at J.R. Snider Ltd. The quote is as follows: "What would Joey do?"

Yep. It's short and sweet. But when my team lived by it, it accomplished two things. It kept them out of trouble and it usually caused them to do things the hard way.

The people who coined that saying are what this section is about.

I had a business coach, one of many, but this one constantly challenged me. He said, "What's all this talk about Snider's Riders, and your constant talk about your core values? Let's let your client base know what makes you tick."

So, I explained to him that the guys and gals referred to themselves as Snider's Riders and it actually became a thing. So, at the prompting of my coach, we put that together with my core values and we came up with a poster titled "DNA of Snider's Riders."

As the company grew, I put a poster together to describe the people that gave me the permission to call myself the Boss. These people have made me proud to say that I'm the Boss.

Then, one day, someone wrote "What would Joey do?" with a permanent marker on my training easel and it just stuck as a saying around the shop.

It's my team who put the meaning in the quote of "What would Joey do?" It's not about whoever Joey is, it's about doing the right thing every time.

Let's describe what some of Snider's Riders look like. I'll start with our Core Values. They are as follows:

- Trust
- Respect
- Understanding
- Credibility
- Kindness
- Humor

Yes, humor is in there, because if you can't laugh at yourself, then you are just too serious—there's a time and a place for everything.

I've had the privilege of working with many different types of people and have learned my fair share from these comrades. I have also been in the position to challenge many people and have rattled many cages to bring them out of their comfort zones. There are always those who are unwilling to leave their comfort zones, but those that are willing to grow, to take the advice and come back for more are what I will refer to as "Snider's Riders."

For example, I'll start with a person I'll call Sarah.

Sarah was a shy young lady that applied for a job while she was finishing up a degree at a local college. She was a little green, yet confident. During the interview my general manager asked her to sit at his desk and take a phone call that (unbeknownst to her) was me on the other end. She answered the phone, and I presented my predicament of no water. She instantly had empathy oozing through the phone. You would have thought she had worked here for years. She accepted our offer of employment the next day.

A year later, it was a cold January weekend when we were absolutely swamped with emergency calls due to frozen and bursting water pipes. I called her in for backup help with the phones. We worked all night and through the entire weekend. It was then that I realized this young lady was not being utilized properly. She has a unique ability to multitask, prevent logistical nightmares, keep customers feeling like they are the only one, and smile while doing it all. She's got intestinal fortitude.

I had fun watching her grow, and she allowed me to rattle her cage and accepted every challenge I threw at her. I remember telling her, "You could go run a Fortune 500 company when you get bored here!" Seventeen years later she decided to move on to another challenge and will take her career to the next level.

Another person who demonstrated the DNA of Snider's Riders I'll refer to as Brad.

This young man is a sponge. He had allowed me to literally throw him from the frying pan into the fire and then he'd come back for more. Over the years he became an exceptional problem solver. His technical skill set and abilities to see the next problem before it happened separated him from many.

I challenged him to become an excellent communicator. I told him that in order to do this, you have to listen twice as much as you talk, in addition to being able to stay calm and focused when the situation gets out of hand.

We had a saying between the two of us, "When everything goes perfectly, we all look good, but when things go south, and you take ownership and put it back together, that's when you see what you're really made of."

As Brad's confidence grew, so did his ability to build trust and credibility. He was treated like a true advisor by our clientele.

The next step on his journey was to meet in person with some unhappy customers. Yes, we made mistakes, and yes, this young man learned to evaluate the situation, put the client as ease, solve the problem and usually return with a request for additional services.

Another invaluable member of the Snider's Riders team is someone we're going to call Chris.

Twenty-plus years ago Chris applied for a job with the understanding that he wanted to start his own plumbing company. He had prior drain cleaning experience and told me he could be a great asset to the company while he learned to be a service plumber. He promised me he'd be loyal and signed up for a three-year apprenticeship.

As time went on, Chris proved to be a man of his word. He'd become a pretty good service plumber. His three years was up, and we met in my office. To my surprise, Chris asked for two more years of employment. I agreed, and back to work we went. Chris went on to develop our septic division, which eventually garnered one-third of our company's revenue.

Some fifteen years later he's still one of Snider's Riders. Not to speak for Chris, but I think he learned there's a lot more than just being a good plumber when it comes to putting up your own sign. Luckily for us, he decided to stay on as a core part of our team.

The stories and list of people who proved their worth as Snider's Riders goes on and on, but the one common denominator that is unmistakable is this: If you as the boss surround yourself with smart people who exhibit the core values of your company, your business will excel and you yourself will become smarter.

ON CALL? WHAT IS THAT?

My Aunt Betty made a needlepoint picture for me years ago. It was a poem that said, "Always on call for whatever arises! When folks need a plumber, it's always a crisis."

So exactly what is "on call" to a service plumber? Sounds easy to answer, but there's a lot involved.

When my wife would start the interview process with a plumber candidate, one of the first questions she asked was, "Have you ever done on-call work?" The answer was usually, "Oh yes, no problem. I'm used to working late and on weekends—been doing it for years!" She was tough on this matter and would reply, "I'm sure you have, but I want you to understand our definition of 'on call' before we move forward."

So, here's what "on" really means in our company. First and foremost, there's no complaining in plumbing.

Your emergency rotation is every 5 weeks. That's 10 times per year. Our emergency service hours are 7:00 AM until 9:00 PM Monday through Saturday, Sunday 7:00 AM until 5:00 PM. When you get a call or text from dispatch, you need to respond within 15 minutes. We provide technical support at all times.

There are times when you feel like you're being left in a difficult situation. You may feel it's a two-man job and will want help, but it's just not available. Unless safety is an issue, we just pull on our boots and get it done.

You will need the support of your family as there will be times that this job will interfere with family activities. We encourage you to be a team player so others will switch on-call duties with you at these times.

We understand the complexity of the on-call duties. The monetary compensation is equal to the efforts we are expecting. If you disagree, please don't accept this job. On-call is a duty that separates the men from the boys and the women from the girls. It's a high level of professionalism that's not for everyone. Our customers always ask me, "Where do you find these types of people?" My response is always the same. "When it's too tough for everyone else, it's just getting right for us."

We lead from the front, not from behind.

BALANCING CAREER AND FAMILY

This profession is not for everyone. And if you decide to pursue this occupation, your loved ones need to be on board and understand you're not always a 9-to-5 guy or gal. Yes, your standard of living has the potential to be very lucrative, but it does come at a cost to family. You can be out working at times that you would usually spend with family, during some weekends and even some holidays.

You must always be a master of priorities to be successful. It's a fine line to walk, but you will learn to build a big bank account *after* you build the emotional bank account with your family.

That's another magic bullet that will make or break you. Show your family they are the most important part of your life so that when you are pulled away at times, they will understand you are working for a better life for them.

It's tough to be on top of your game when you feel guilty about your absence or have an angry spouse to come home to—you have to have their support and understanding. And when you do, you will be even more successful both personally and professionally.

Every job and career has its challenges, and one of the biggest challenges today is the work-life balance and the fact that most households have two careers going on at the same time. There are child-care issues as well as finding quality family time. Sounds impossible to be a service plumber and a good family man or family woman too, doesn't it?

Well, let's go back and look at the ingredients of a professional service provider. If you have passion and dedication, you will be an asset wherever you choose to work. Your core values will be a compass that will keep you moving in the right direction. Your willingness and respectfulness will gain you trust and credibility with a company that will gladly work with you to provide a job that has the flexibility for a good work-life balance and security for your future. I've just described a win-win situation for both you and your employer. This person is what every owner is looking for, and you are worth your weight in gold. So yes, it is very possible to be a service plumber and a good family man or family woman at the same time.

FRONTLINE STORIES: NEVER A DULL MOMENT

TO FLUSH OR NOT TO FLUSH

This short story is a list of things I have removed from water closets (toilets) over the years. I'm never surprised at what is considered by some to be flushable.

Here's my top ten list of items that did not make it through the loo!!

- A mouse trap (and yes, the mouse was still attached)
- Reading glasses
- Toilet paper holder tube with the spring
- Perfume bottles
- Pot pipes
- G.I. Joe figurines
- Popsicle sticks

- Hygiene products
- Makeup mirrors
- And ... last but not least ... a wallet in a public men's room. (Yes, it was a little dingy but returned to its rightful out-of-state owner.)

LESSON LEARNED

If you drop something in the loo, it's okay to reach in and retrieve it. It won't hurt you. We plumbers are living proof. But it's okay because it's all in a day's work for a service plumber.

A PS on the wallet example is that the gentleman didn't even realize it had dropped out of his trousers when he sat down and he was flabbergasted when it was returned. (And you bet he gave a good tip!!!)

ALL IN A DAY'S WORK

Sometimes life throws things at you to see what you are made of. We serviced many large farms in the area. One day my brother and I were digging up a water hydrant in the center aisleway of a show barn for cattle. We heard the barn manager yell for help. We both dropped our shovels and went to see what he needed.

He said grab the ends of those two braided chains. My brother is an EMT volunteer and basically pushed me aside and followed the instructions of the barn manager. Well, about a half hour later they delivered two baby calves. The manager had to blow into the nose of the second-born calf to get her breathing. Mom and babies were fine. We finished our hydrant replacement and had a story to tell!

LESSON LEARNED

Keep your cool, know when to follow instructions and know when to get out of the way!!

D.I.Y.

Over the years I had the privilege of working for many prestigious people. One of these clients was hosting a fundraiser for Bill Clinton. Her farm manager called me to install a water feature that was picked out and he wanted it installed in the koi pond below the terrace garden. So, with a small johnboat we installed the water feature.

A few days later Bill (the farm manager) called and said they had purchased a different water feature and could we please come and remove the one we'd installed and put this new one in its place. After the second feature was installed, it didn't meet the expectations of the owners. One of my plumbers told the manager, jokingly, that we could make a better fountain than the ones that were purchased.

Joke or no joke, Bill asked me to make a water feature that was not too loud but still had an arch of 20 feet and three different circumferences.

So, I went to the plumber who had the brilliant idea and said, "Okay, Mike, you have authorization to make a water feature."

Mike got right to work. Outfitted with a 60-foot roll of 2-inch soft copper and several dozen grease fittings (a fitting used to apply grease to a bearing on heavy equipment) and the same number of ¼-inch throttling valves, he said, "Leave me alone at the shop for one day and I'll be ready to deliver it to the pond."

The water feature was installed; a dedicated booster pump was piped into the loop. After balancing the water flow through the grease fittings with the throttling valves, it met all criteria. It was 25 feet high, 40 feet radius, and three beautiful columns of tranquil water.

The owners were so impressed that we were asked to attend the gala. Not as guests, but as water feature attendants. We were there to make sure the fountain operated perfectly during the event. And yes, we were background checked and escorted at all times with our own Secret Service agents during the event.

LESSON LEARNED

If you don't put "blinders" on yourself or those around you, the opportunities we are presented with are endless! It's easy to become complacent and say, "That's not my job!" Likewise, it's difficult to challenge yourself when you really don't have to. But those few who do become the best of the best.

OUT OF SIGHT FOR NOW!

At the conclusion of a drain-cleaning call for a stopped-up main sewer line, the man of the house came out to see what caused the blockage.

My helper was cleaning off the retriever head on the electric drain snake. He said, "No worries, Mr. Customer, it was just some condoms that got caught in an elbow just before the septic tank. We have used a camera to inspect the entire sewer system and you are all clear."

He replied, "That's impossible! I don't use condoms."

Needless to say, we collected our payment quickly and headed to our next call.

LESSON LEARNED

Mr. Customer was either in denial or else had a few sleepless nights figuring out how those got in there. Unfortunately, it was a case of out of sight but not out of mind!!

JEWELED FAUCETS AND GOLD-PLATED SINKS

I had a longtime customer call me and ask for a service call to install new fixtures in her powder room.

When I arrived, Mrs. Gardener asked me if I ever installed plumbing fixtures from Sherle Wagner International.

I replied, "No, but that sounds fancy. Let's take a look!"

We opened some heavily-foamed packed crates to find a gold widespread lavatory faucet. The spout was a glorious swan, and the handles were laden with real emeralds. The pedestal sink was gold-plated porcelain. Even the toilet handle had emeralds embedded in the porcelain. The toilet handle was painted with gold edges and swirls.

Here I am looking at these fixtures and I ask, "Are those real?" Mrs. Gardener said, "Yes, they better be for what they cost!!"

I didn't dare ask how much they cost, I just said I couldn't give her a fixed price on the job but would gladly do it on a time and materials basis. She said as long as I was doing the work, she would agree.

We agreed to pick a Saturday when I would have no distractions and Mrs. Gardener would be away at a horse show.

I started unpacking everything and told myself, "It's just regular plumbing fixtures. It's just a toilet and a pedestal lavatory. No big deal."

After 9 or 10 hours of tediously and cautiously assembling parts and pieces, I finally used a small Allen wrench to put the finishing touches on the handles of both faucet and toilet. Then I cut the closet bolts flush with the gold-painted toilet base and put the solid gold bolt covers on.

Yes, I was done!!

I tested my connections. I polished the gold, emeralds, and porcelain just in time for Mrs. Gardener to return with her friends to celebrate their blue-ribbon winnings from the horse show!

While I was putting my tools away, Mrs. Gardener walked me out on my final trip. It was then that she told me what the fixtures cost!

Good thing she waited to share that number!

LESSON LEARNED

Don't avoid things that aren't in your wheelhouse. When you have the opportunity to work out of your comfort zone, embrace the challenge.

I remember feeling intimidated at the beginning of the installation, but by the end of the day I had realized that it's just a frame of mind. I came away with a newfound confidence—not in a conceited or brash sense but more of a low-key anticipation of "What's next?!!"

LEAK DETECTION —HONDA STYLE

I was on a no-water call with my father one summer day. I was 13 years old. It was a huge farm, and the main water supply came from a very large concrete reservoir that was filled by a spring coming out of the mountainside. There were literally miles of underground pipes that were used to gravity feed all the livestock troughs.

We drove the truck around all the usual fields where previous repairs had been made but found no leaks. I said, "Dad, what are we going to do now? The truck won't go up those fire trails." He said, "There's still miles of pipes to check, but I have an idea." No more was said; we just left the job and went home.

I was very puzzled. Even though it was the end of the workday, my father didn't ever leave people or animals without water if there was anything he could do about it. So, we pull into our driveway and Dad says, "Go get your QA50" (a small Honda mini-bike). I said, "Okay. But what for?" Dad said, "You are going to find the leak on the mountain."

Oh my gosh! You can only imagine the excitement in my voice despite trying to be cool and calm. Not only was I going to be really helping my dad, but I'd be getting paid to ride my dirt bike!

We returned to the cattle farm and with a full tank of gas and explicit instructions I was off as proud as I could be. About half an hour into my trail riding, I came across a small stream of water running down the hillside. I parked my bike and followed the stream to find a spurting waterfall coming from the broken gravity water main. I returned to my father with hands waving and a big smile. "I found it, Dad! I found it!"

The farm manager brought my dad and his tools as close as possible with a small tractor and we walked the rest of the way to make the necessary repairs.

After the water was restored, the farm manager told my dad he could bring me over anytime to ride the trails and "keep an eye on the water pipes."

LESSON LEARNED

You never know how your actions can affect other people in your life. I'm sure there was a much more efficient way of locating that leak, but to this day I remember how proud I was and how important I felt. I'll continue to pay it forward and treat others just like I was treated.

PART THREE

BLUE-COLLAR VERSUS
WHITE-COLLAR

LET'S COMPARE THE TWO

I n today's job market I find it both fascinating and concerning when the topic of blue-collar versus white-collar comes up.

I'll start by stating the obvious: Blue-collar workers perform physical labor while white-collar workers perform intellectual labor. That sounds simple and clear-cut, doesn't it? That's what causes the misconception held by many people that are entering the job market.

Let me share my interpretation of a blue-collar tradesman in contrast with a white-collar professional. We'll start out with hypothetical examples of a high school graduate in both cases.

In the blue-collar world, you go through an apprenticeship program that is referred to as OTJT (on-the-job training) or "earn as you learn." This consists of both a regular daytime job working with a master in your chosen trade as well as evening classroom curriculum to obtain the necessary continuing educational credits you will need to sit for your journeyman's and master's licenses.

This process is best suited for an individual with very little personal debt, as the entry-level pay rate is low. The upside is that in two to three years you will be a journeyman and making a better than average living with no student loans. Then, after you have your journeyman's license and the required formal training credits, you can sit for your master's licensing. Your state department of professional and occupational regulation agency (DPOR) will explain the exact requirements for your location and trade.

Once you have your master's in your chosen trade, you are among the best of the best, and your pay scale should reflect your accomplishments and abilities. So, let's say you graduate high school at 18 years of age and get a job with a reputable company that provides plumbing and HVAC services. You surround yourself with tradesmen and you are a sponge. One day your boss calls you into his or her office. They ask you how serious you are about staying in the trades and would you consider going to a local community college for the formal training necessary to become a journeyman. If you comply and pass the courses, all expenses are company-paid. And yes, it's obvious that they expect some loyalty on your part.

Now you're 21 years of age and you have your journeyman's card. That's a huge accomplishment. Your pay scale and benefits will reflect your efforts. Then another two years later, you sit for your master's license.

Now you're not even 25 years old and you have an established career path and a high-paying job. As long as you didn't buy a bunch of toys as your income increased, you should have a decent savings account and no student loans to pay off.

With the credentials listed above at the age of 23 to 25, your yearly income bracket should be $60K to $150K depending on your market and the amount of skin you are willing to put in the game. With a company retirement match of 3% to 6% and health insurance contributions, you may be earning a salary comparable to many executives.

After some years in the field, you may find yourself at a crossroads and go into a supervisory or management position. These positions have salaries that meet and beat the salaries of many owners in the industry. The opportunities and salaries are available to meet your lifestyle standards in the trades. It's just a matter of getting in young, not becoming complacent, and becoming a sponge.

As with anything in life, you get what you give. And with any lucrative position comes additional responsibilities and the challenges of the work-life balance.

Now on to my perspective of the white-collar world.

You are 17 years old, in your senior year of high school, and you start applying to the colleges of your choice. You either get accepted to a 4-year college, or you sign up for community college to get your GPA up to speed. At the age of 22 or 23 you have a bachelor's degree, let's say in business administration and entrepreneurial management, or perhaps an accounting or an engineering degree. You sign up for a 2-year MBA program, and at age 24 or 25 you have your MBA.

You are now entering the job market at age 24 to 25. You may have student loans that vary from $100K to $200K. You graduated in the top 5% of your class and you get job offers from several firms across the country. You accept a job at a local engineering firm. Your starting yearly salary is $80K. A year later and you have been assigned better projects as well as increases in salary and benefits now totaling $90K. Six months later you receive an offer extended from an executive recruiter from a competitor for $100K plus relocation expenses. Now you're a player in your field. Your new firm has many opportunities for you to grow.

Now you're 26 to 27 years old and living in the suburbs with a 30-minute commute and working from home two days out of five. You are reaping the benefits of your higher education. In the gym at 6:00 AM, to work by 8:00 AM, and home by 6:00 PM.

By the age of 30 you are pushing $150K plus benefits, putting you in the $175K salary bracket.

For the sake of my comparison, let's stop tracking both of these careers at age 30. Also, let's remember that I am presenting this example based on my experience as a blue-collar worker and an owner of a small to mid-sized plumbing and water treatment company.

Let us now do a comparison on the higher education route versus on-the-job training (OTJT).

In my opinion, to become a good technician, it takes five years of on-the-job training. During these five years an apprenticeship school program is completed with 240 hours of classroom time—usually in the evenings one to two days per week from 6:00 PM to 9:00 PM. At this point, you're qualified to test for your master's licensure in most localities.

Not so for the higher education received at a college or university. A bachelor's degree is usually received in 4 years of study and a master's degree is completed in one to two more years. So, for the sake of argument, let's say 5 years and you have a master's degree in engineering.

Now both candidates are 23 years old. The blue-collar candidate is a full-fledged plumbing technician and has applied to the state of residence for his or her master plumbing and gas licenses. The white-collar candidate has just graduated with his or her master's in engineering.

Let's discuss the cost of obtaining a skill set versus a college degree. This example assumes that both parties have to pay their own way.

The blue-collar worker enters the workforce in an entry-level position and a very low hourly pay rate with, generally speaking, no benefits. This is the nature of the beast and why I stated it's only sustainable when you are young and have very little debt.

A very meager standard of living for the upcoming apprentice might be an understatement. After two years, the apprentice will start to see light at the end of the tunnel. Yes, it takes time even if you are a quick study. So now your income is reasonable, and if you don't stay disciplined, you can easily become complacent.

This two-year point is a crossroads in the trades, especially in today's world. I mentioned earlier that my generation had a three-year apprenticeship working with masters of the trade almost every day. The apprentice today is usually put out on his or her own at two years of training. I saw it often; these young people don't have the exposure to the old work ethic. They feel like they are being left high and dry and as I've heard them say, "The juice isn't worth the squeeze."

It may seem like I'm getting off track here, but this is the cost of obtaining a skill set. You must pay your dues. If it was easy, you would have a lot of competition.

At this point in your journey you'll have to take a look around. If you're complaining because you are not appreciated and feel taken for granted, then do something about it, but don't quit.

When I was young, I had the opportunity to work with excellent tradesmen and saw the lifestyle they lived. If your morale is flagging, take a look in the mirror and ask yourself this question: "Where do I want to be in three years and how do I get there?"

The cost of not having a goal is hard to measure, but setting goals and having a plan to get there gives you the purpose and drive necessary to get through the tough process of becoming a master of your trade. The true cost of tuition for a blue-collar worker is the investment you put into yourself—your classroom is your job. The fruits of your labor are right around the corner, and don't forget, you are only 25 or 26 years old! Maybe you're even fresh out of high school, which is even better timing!

So now to the cost of what we refer to as "higher education." Our candidate has a master's in engineering.

He or she just graduated and has sent their resume out to multiple firms. We will use a figure of $175K in student loans to pay back. This candidate graduated in the top 10% of the class and has two offers of employment within a month of graduating. The job our candidate accepts pays $88K per year plus relocation expenses with a two-year commitment. So off they go and instantly put their education to work.

Don't forget, our candidate has five years of classroom education and constant testing and exams to prove that they have retained the necessary information to be an engineer. Theirs is a full-time commitment to receive a master's in engineering in 5 years. Plus the cost of tuition, books, room and board. Talk about paying your dues! This is a tough 5 years.

At this point the white-collar worker immediately catches up to the blue-collar worker's salary. But let's not forget the student loans that have to be accounted for.

Our white-collar candidate excelled during their two-year commitment and received a salary increase of 6% per year, which puts him or her at 93K per year. This candidate has earned the trust and respect from the boss to work from home two days per week and commute three days.

So, what's the actual cost for a master's degree in engineering? Well, let's assume the $175K in student loans takes care of tuition, books, and incidentals. There's still room and board and transportation. Our candidate worked a part-time job on campus to cover these expenses. That doesn't leave any time to participate in any other extracurricular college activities.

As you can see, there are trade-offs no matter which route you decide to commit to. And it could be argued that after that initial five-year commitment, going into the trades has a similar financial payoff to going into a professional career. It's just a matter of deciding what your personal priorities, interests and aptitudes are. Can you picture yourself being challenged by and deriving satisfaction from a sedentary desk job or a more physically demanding trade?

Only you can decide whether the effort to attain either goal is worth it to you personally.

THE "BLUE-COLLAR REVOLUTION"

In our world today, working as a trade laborer has gotten some negative press, and white-collar workers have more cultural capital. However, I think it's extremely important to address the shrinking skilled labor workforce entering the trades and what opportunities that presents for young people entering the workforce today.

I consider myself qualified to discuss the advances, changes and opportunities available for people who are entering the workplace or perhaps unhappy with where they are in their career.

I will start with a common piece of advice that many parents offer their children as they approach their senior year in high school: "You've got to go to college to get a good job."

There was a time when this was pretty sound advice for most high schoolers. But back then the cost of a college degree was much more financially palatable and a 4-year bachelor's degree was considered higher education. In today's world, a bachelor's degree doesn't have the same level of prestige, and the need to obtain a master's degree to compete seems to be the new standard. That's usually 6 to 7 years of study after high school.

When I was in high school, there were two paths to choose. There were AP classes (advanced placement) for those pursuing college and shop class for those who were not interested in higher education and who perhaps had a lower GPA.

Back 40 years ago when I entered the plumbing trade, it was much more labor-intensive. We were using threading machines for steel pipe, cast iron cutters, pouring lead joints and soldering copper pipes. Everything was painstakingly heavy and at times monotonous, to be perfectly honest. Those of us called old-timers learned our trades and things didn't really change much. We were working in a time when the materials and techniques for installation remained consistent for many years. Then came the introduction of new types of materials to our industry. No more heavy steel, cast iron, or copper pipes. Now there's PVC, ABS, CPVC, and CSST to replace the old pipe and fittings we had used for 75 years.

Now we have tankless water heaters, modulating well pumps, residential macerating sewage pumps, and toilets that flush with just over a gallon of water. The tools of the trade have changed, and so have the people performing the work.

I consider myself privileged to have been part of this evolution in the plumbing industry.

PLUMBING TECHNICIANS HAVE MANY SKILL SETS

Today's people in the trades are referred to as "technicians" and rightfully so. The nature of the beast has changed and so have many other aspects of being in the trades.

This person must be able to understand and able to work with the steel, cast iron and copper pipes described above as well as stay on top of the ever-changing technological advancements. Everything is Wi-Fi compatible, from your water heater to your water softener.

The salary and benefit packages for today's technician are mind-blowing. The skill set is both mechanical and technical. The new blue-collar worker is using both their back *and* their brain. That sounds like a very rewarding career to me.

As we know, the need for toilets, sinks, showers, and sanitary facilities for bathing and cooking will go on forever. So too will the need for those people who install and maintain such fixtures and the infrastructure for these facilities.

For those who realize that technology has revolutionized the blue-collar job description, the world is at your fingertips. Yes, you still need to use your hands and your back to some degree, but you have a job where you are challenged both mentally and physically.

Here's a perfect example of my point. A tankless water heater weighs in at 25 to 40 pounds and hangs on the wall like a heavy mirror. After the basic pipe connections are completed is when the real work starts. Wiring up the motherboard, presetting the dip switches for the proper application, perhaps setting up a small manifold of units that operate in series or in parallel.

This industry needs people willing to work with both their hands and their minds. Very soon most plumbing fixtures will be touchless with Wi-Fi capabilities. Who's going to be able to install and maintain these new products that will make our lives better? I can honestly say that my knowledge as a master plumber, gas fitter, alternative septic systems and water well provider will soon be only half of what will be needed.

This revolution I speak of can't be defined by the color of a collar in my opinion but if a color has to be given, I'd call it a green-collar job, not just because of being environmentally friendly but also because of the salary it will demand for the first in line who aren't afraid of the challenges awaiting the new tradesman!

FRONTLINE STORIES: FAR FROM THE BORING OFFICE

THE ULTIMATE PAYBACK...

During my new construction days, I was on a job where multiple houses were being constructed and there were many trades on site.

One day I was on a roof putting a flashing on a vent pipe when I saw a guy go into the Don's John (portable toilet). Then a fellow came out of a truck beside the John with a roll of duct tape and wrapped the tape several times around the entire unit so the door would not open. He pulled out a tow strap and wrapped it around the portable toilet, attached the other end to a trailer hitch on his bumper, and proceeded to pull this poor fellow around the cul-de-sac inside the portable toilet until it tipped over. Then he stopped the truck, cut the tape, rolled up his tow strap, and left.

Later it was determined to be a jealous husband retaliating for his wife's betrayal.

LESSON LEARNED
Well, I think we all know this one, so I'll leave it at that.

SIDE WORK

As the company grew and more trucks were on the road, I decided to be one of the first in my area to put GPS in the service vans.

I had one particular plumber who called in sick more than normal. One day he called in sick again and something didn't feel quite right.

Back then the GPS wasn't actually live but would download the travel of that vehicle when it was within sight of an antenna on our building. So, he came back to work, and I noticed his van had moved while he was off sick.

It appeared he had gone to do a side job while he was "sick"—using the company van, tools and materials.

I went to the address he'd gone to and talked to the homeowners. They were very understanding of the situation and informed me he planned to come finish on Sunday. If I let him finish, they would find an excuse not to be there and I could make a visit.

This gets better. They also promised they would pay *me* the amount agreed to instead of him.

So, I agreed. I waited until midday Sunday, walked into the basement and hollered, "Plumbing inspector!"

Well, we both looked at each other and he said, "Damn, I guess that new GPS thing really works!!"

I said, "Unfortunately for you, yes it does."

I fired him on the spot and everything ended peacefully. But it was somewhat of an awkward hour while we waited together for his wife to come pick him up.

LESSON LEARNED
Trust your gut.

THE JACK RUSSELL

A call came in that a customer named Mrs. Smith needed us to find a Jack Russell puppy that possibly went down into a groundhog hole.

I called Mrs. Smith back and explained that she would need to call animal control. She was crying on the phone and said that someone told her to call us as we had a sewer camera that would fit into the holes. She begged us to see if the puppy was in one of several possible groundhog holes.

So off we went with our sewer camera and a portable generator. When we arrive, Mrs. Smith, her granddaughter, and the barn manager are all gathered around these holes. We got the camera operating and went down into several holes. The only thing we saw was one scared groundhog.

Then, in the very last hole we investigated, there was the puppy! It was curled up in a little ball and shivering, probably three to four feet down in the ground.

Long story short, we put peanut butter on a napkin, zip-tied it to the camera, and watched the little puppy follow it to the entrance to the hole. Mrs. Smith's granddaughter picked him up safe and sound.

LESSON LEARNED

You never know how much publicity you can get from a kind gesture. The word "viral" wasn't a thing at that time, but I received a lot of good press!

HEFTY BAGS

Working in a small town, you pretty much know many of your customers personally. Many times, you'd find a note on the door saying, "Snider people, come on in, I'll be home later. Just leave the invoice on the kitchen counter." This was the case for this visit.

I finished replacing a garbage disposal and a leaking P-trap under the sink. I cleaned up my mess and used the customer's trash can to dispose of my trash. Her trash can was almost full, so I put a new plastic bag in her trash can and took the full bag with me as the courteous thing to do. I left my invoice on the counter and was off to my next call.

The next morning, I received a frantic phone message: "Joey, this is Mrs. B. My trash is missing. Did you take it? Please call me back immediately!"

I returned her call to explain what I had done, and she was very upset and told me I needed to return her trash ASAP.

I drove back to the shop, praying that our dumpster hadn't been emptied yet. Upon arrival I found that the dumpster was still full. Whew! I scavenged through the dumpster and found the trash bag, still tied up just like I left it.

I returned to Mrs. B's house to find her waiting in the driveway almost in tears. She tore the bag open and retrieved an empty jelly jar with a paper towel inside. She unwrapped the paper towel and out came her wedding rings.

"This is my hiding place," she told me. She explained that she puts the rings in the jar when she's doing dishes. Her husband thought it was an empty jar and threw it away.

What are the chances of this chain of events? The perfect storm, is all I can say.

LESSON LEARNED
Bring your own trash bags on all future service calls.

NEW YEAR'S EVE AT THE B&B

It's New Year's Eve and a call from a local B&B comes in. Stopped-up toilet.

I arrive and speak with the GM. She is checking in a couple and tells me, "Room number 4. Second floor. Mr. Doe is rather upset. I'll follow right behind you."

I head off in the direction of the rooms, knock on door number 4 and holler, "Plumber!"

A voice answers, "Come in," so I enter the room.

I holler, "Plumber!" again.

A voice replies, "I'm in here, come on in," so I open the door to the bedroom.

A scream of "You're not Harry!" rings out and I instantly close the door.

I met the GM and Harry in the hallway. GM says, "Oh my gosh! It was room number 3, not number 4!"

Harry hands me the bottle of champagne he'd left to get and said, "I won't be needing this."

LESSON LEARNED

This story gives a new meaning to the phrase "Happy New Year!!"

WEDDING BAND ADVENTURES

One of my plumbers in the septic and drain-cleaning division had recently gotten married.

One day, not long after his honeymoon, he was in the process of completing an evaluation on an effluent pump and floats when he called me to let me know that his wedding band had come off his hand and dropped into the effluent tank. He assured me, in no uncertain terms, that his new bride would not be very understanding of the situation.

I headed over to join him and we put the control box in manual to pump down to the last 6 inches of wastewater. Then we put on Tyvek suits, rubber boots and gloves, and scoured every inch of the bottom until his ring was retrieved.

I hope that marriage lasts!!

LESSON LEARNED

I use a variation of the 80/20 rule for this one: Life is 20% what happened and 80% how you reacted.

MY ELECTRIC BILL IS TOO HIGH!

We put an electric water heater in a tenant house for a landlord. A month later the landlord called and told us that after we installed the new tank, her electric bill skyrocketed. She was convinced it must be the new water heater.

I went by to check out the amperage and voltage on the new heater. All was normal, but I noticed a strange light under the cellar door.

To my surprise, I found multiple purple growing lights throughout the boiler room. I informed the landlord that the tenants must be growing "tomatoes" in the basement and the purple lights were the reason for the higher-than-normal electrical consumption!

LESSON LEARNED

There's a time to just mind your own business!!

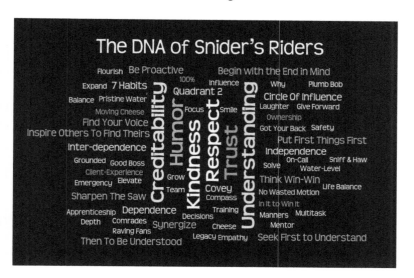

Some of Snider's Riders installing individual supply and return hydronic heat lines in the crawlspace of an old mansion. Pictured Josh (left) and Sammy (right).

Emma and Ryan, the next generation of "Snider's Riders".

My view on an early-morning ride before work.

An article on our company that ran in the local Middleburg magazine.

If Water Runs Through It, We Do It!

Kyle replacing an effluent distribution box for the septic system on a large estate in Virginia.

My father, Ray Snider, 1931-2017

All hands on deck! Our operation manager, Sarah, and office manager, Kristi, jump in to deliver parts to technicians on an especially busy day.

With Scarlett the pig. Taken during a service visit to the owner's farm.

The water treatment system for a large farm. This one was situated in an underground vault.

At the Home and Garden show in D.C., networking and promoting the business. Pictured L-R: Brad, Sammy, Joey, Joey Snider, along with my dog Jesse James.

Riding my show horse, Pallas Jäger, as we finished a cross-country race.

One of our wrapped vans.

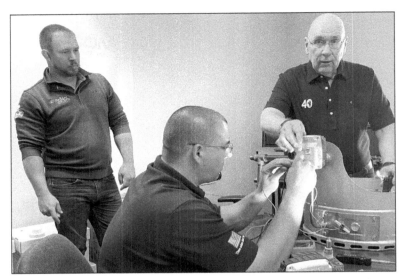

In class, learning how to connect water heaters to Wi-Fi. An example of what a new technician needs to know. Pictured L-R: Brad, Joey, technical support instructor.

Joey & Sarah, the operations manager at a home show.

PART FOUR

WHAT DOES IT TAKE TO BE THE OWNER?

SO YOU REALLY WANT TO BE AN ENTREPRENEUR?

B y this point in the book, you might be wondering whether it'd be better to be the owner of a service business rather than the service plumber employed by someone else. It's a valid question.

Let's start by defining what we mean by the word entrepreneur:

"A person who organizes and operates a business, taking on greater than normal financial risks in order to do so."

Organizing a business, operating a business, and taking on greater than normal financial risks—that's what an aspiring entrepreneur is signing up for.

But nuts and bolts of ownership are still too vague. So, here's a possible hypothetical scenario. Imagine that I am a young man who has acquired all the licensing necessary to open my own plumbing company. I am currently employed by a very well-run company and making a salary of $125K plus profit sharing and benefits, which puts me at roughly $160K.

I am working an average of 45 hours per week, and I'm on call once every five weeks. I generate an average of $10K to $15K per week for my employer, some weeks much more than that. That's over half a million dollars in business revenue each and every year.

At times it seems like my share of that pot is unfair for what I do.

The guy that owns this place comes in at 11:00 AM, leaves at 4:00 PM, and just walks around whistling while he is here. Seems like an easy way to make a lot of money. I know he does a lot behind the scenes, but how difficult can it really be? I'm working as hard or harder than the boss and don't have anything close to what he has. I think it's time for me to take the plunge and start making real money before I'm past my prime!!

So, I talk to my wife and try to convince her that I'm going to nearly double my income.

She's skeptical and asks how.

"It's pretty simple," I explain. "Right now, my hourly pay rate averages $55 per hour. I know I can charge $135 per hour if I'm out on my own. That's more than twice what I'm making now even after I hire my existing helper away from the company. It's a no-brainer. The boss has tons of overhead that I won't have, and can you imagine the money we will have if I only do half of the weekly gross that I'm doing for him? That's over a quarter of a million dollars! And what if I *do* make half a million for us instead of him? We deserve all the fruits of my labor. I'm putting in my two weeks' notice tomorrow."

Let's fast-forward six months and imagine that I am sitting down with my wife, who takes care of the books. She's concerned about the balance of funds in our business checking account.

She begins, "So … we took $10,000 out of our savings to get the business started and we paid it back a couple of months ago just like you said we would. That's great, but we just received an invoice for the remaining balance of our general liability and auto policies. It's $4,500. Plus, the bills for materials were more than normal. Which invoice do you want me to pay? If we pay both, we'll need to dip back into the savings we just recouped."

I explain that a couple of really big jobs are almost done, and the money will be coming in, so just pay both and everything will be fine in two weeks.

Two weeks fly by and the money from those jobs lands in the account. All is going well. We are rolling in the dough.

Then my wife comes to me with a look of concern. "I met with our accountant today to see what she needs to prepare for our year-end income tax report. She asked for our A/R (accounts receivable), A/P (accounts payable), and so on. I had everything she needed."

"But then," my wife goes on, "she asked me for our quarterly payment schedule and the amount of each payment. I told her we hadn't made any quarterly payments. 'Oh my!' she told me. 'You'll have to make it up with one lump sum, and then we'll get you on track for next year. The next quarterly payment is April 15th along with this year's taxes, so that's going to be a doozy of a check. But the next quarterly payment isn't until June 15th, so you will have two months to recover.'"

Our accountant later explained to us that when you are an employee, your employer pays half of your Social Security and Medicare taxes. But when you are self-employed (as we are now), you pay the entire tax amount yourself.

That's an extra 7% to 8% in taxes on our dime!

So now it's April. We've paid our tax bill and our savings are depleted. On the bright side, we have plenty of work, and moving forward, we have a Certified Public Accountant to work with.

Now that we've put that lesson behind us, I'm working six days per week to get the safety net built back up in our savings account. I celebrated my first full year of being in business for myself. Time flies when you are having fun, and I am excited to meet with our CPA and go over my financial reports.

Here's a summary of yearly financials:

My gross receipts totaled $350,000. Not bad for my first year and just getting my name out there.

Then come the expense reports. There's the truck payment, general liability and auto insurance, worker's compensation, payroll taxes (and it's only me and my apprentice), supply house invoices, fuel, vehicle maintenance, phone and internet for the office, county and state business licensing and permit fees.

There's also health insurance (the full amount, not 50%), and now that I'm not on a group health plan, my rates and deductibles are higher. Not to forget the rental equipment fees, accountant and legal fees, a small advertising budget for social media, tool, and equipment expenses (such as drain cleaning machines, pump pulling equipment, core and hammer drills, and so on). Next year a sewer camera is on the wish list.

I can't believe how much this all adds up to. Back when I was an employee, my old boss supplied everything except our basic hand and battery tools.

But my accountant isn't through yet. There is a column for "employee burden" that shocks me as I only have one employee who makes $22 per hour. Then there's another column for "lost revenue and customer shrinkage." What the heck is that!? Well, sometimes you either don't get paid for your services or you have to reduce the price in order to get paid.

When I worked for the boss, that was never an issue, or at least not that I was aware of.

Then my accountant informs me, "There were four customers that cost the business for repairs that were so ridiculous I couldn't make a claim to your insurance, so I just paid the invoices forwarded to you from their landscaper, their painter, their carpet cleaning company, and finally their flagstone repair mason."

That reminds me that there are other one-off expenses to tally. For example, my homeowners' association (HOA) complained about me running a plumbing company out of my garage, so I had to rent a storage bay to operate out of for now, and that's $2,400 per year. My apprentice dropped my iPad. $800 gone. Then there's that darn Verizon wireless bill for two cell phones, a laptop, and one (now deceased) iPad. I used my company phone and iPad before and just took it for granted. On top of that, I had to pay the deductible on two cracked windshields and one parking lot fender bender that was nobody's fault (my apprentice says *they* backed into *him!*).

After looking at the credit card processing fees, I'm ready for a cold beer.

Now for the final tally, which I'm told is called the "net profit." In regular terms some people call it disposable income, and if your quarterly tax payments are estimated properly, then I've been told this is the real number you can believe.

I cannot believe that, despite how hard I worked, after the dust has settled I've made $6,500 *less* than I did working for the boss! Plus, I worked most Saturdays and holidays and promised my family a vacation—that has now been postponed indefinitely.

"This cannot be true!" I tell my CPA. "I can't do this for another year!"

She sees the disappointment on my face. She asks me if she can ask me a couple of questions.

"Please," I reply.

"My first question is this: Why did you want to start your own business? Secondly, since you now have an idea of what it takes to make your old salary, do you have the entrepreneurial spirit necessary to expand your business, charge forward and meet these challenges every day, and increase your gross profits so that your net profit meets the financial goals you've set?"

I'm in a quandary. I tell her I can only answer her first question at this point. She asks me to share my answer as a friend to a friend.

I tell her I had great expectations of doing what my old boss did. He ran 7 to 12 service vans, and for the most part everything was good. He was always in a good mood, had a high standard of living, walked around whistling and joking around with everyone. Who wouldn't want that job? It just looked like we were doing all the work, making and collecting all the money, and he just counted it. I wanted that for my family, so that's why I did it.

As far as answering question two, I must digest the fact that unless I run a service company with multiple trucks, employees, and an actual place of business, I'm not going to realize my financial dreams. I just don't know if I want to deal with all the daily, weekly, and quarterly aspects that go into running a successful service company. On top of that is the financial planning and being responsible for other people's livelihoods. It's much more work than I ever imagined.

She stops me right there and recites a saying from the Dalai Lama: "Judge your success by what you had to give up in order to get it."

Those words resonate with me immediately. I realize that my definition of success needs to be redefined.

I realize that, as an employee, I was an extremely successful service plumber. I was a trusted advisor and built trust and credibility with all who knew me. I had learned my trade from some hardcore old-timers. I had worked hard to get to that point. So perhaps I'm not cut out to be the owner of a service company, but instead I am cut out to be an integral part of a successful company.

I don't know if I would have understood this fully without going through the last year, but I do now.

Fast-forward a bit, and let me tell you, it's nice to be back with my old company. I'm happy with what I gave up in order to get what I have. There's room to grow, make a fabulous living, and enjoy being successful every day.

This hypothetical story plays over and over in the trades. It highlights the gritty realities of what it takes to go that extra step and become an owner. Hopefully it helps people think about what they are signing up for before they take that leap of faith.

For those who are still feeling compelled to embark on the owner journey despite the challenges, read on for more of my own personal experience being an owner.

ADOPTING AN OWNER'S MINDSET

So, now I'll play the part of the owner and portray this journey from the standpoint of my eight years as an employee and 39 years as an owner of a plumbing and water treatment company.

For me, the primary reason to become an owner wasn't the owner's salary, but rather a desire to start a company that worked because of synergy and interdependence.

It began in my early days with a concept I learned from my dad: "avoiding wasted motion." It started when my father would ask me why I went back to the truck empty-handed to get something we needed now.

He'd say, "You knew we were done with that drill, why not put it away during a necessary trip to the truck?" If I wanted to see the look of disgust from my dad, then all I had to do was walk to or from my job site with empty hands!

Well, this thing my dad called "wasted motion" became an obsession with me. I took it as a personal challenge to make every step, and everything I did, count twice! I applied it to everything I did.

As I continued in my career, this obsession built a type of frustration inside of me that I couldn't do anything about. This was the driving force behind my determination to become an owner. I could use my logistical mindset to its fullest potential. I knew I could do more with less. I saw it on all the job sites I worked on. I started seeing the wasted motion everywhere I went, even at the grocery store.

Then, when I bought into the business and became an owner, I was always trying to maximize everyone's time, eliminate backtracking, and keep downtime to a bare minimum. Simply working smarter, not harder.

To be an owner without a vision is a disaster waiting to happen. My vision was a well-run company that itself created an environment that was conducive to high productivity and a great place to work. Even at the beginning of my career I paid attention to people and how they reacted to different situations. I looked around all the time to see how we could do things in a more productive manner. I found myself leading the conversations with customers even when I was a plumber's helper.

Another thing I've always tried to do as a business owner is to be of value to others. With a good leader, the customer should already be treated like royalty! But beyond that, whether I was with a client or an employee (and yes, my family), I made my decisions whenever possible based on this theory of adding value. Am I making their life easier? If so, I'll be providing value and be on their priority list. Adding value to others might sound simple, but it's harder than it seems. I kept my eyes on the prize most of the time and consider this particular trait to be very important to my success professionally and personally.

There is one flaw in my approach, and that is that some people will look at you, the boss, and mistake your kindness for weakness. But things get sorted out and understood quickly when owners are able to assert themselves.

Henry Ford famously said, "A business that focuses solely on service will have but one concern with profits. They will be embarrassingly large." This speaks volumes about the mindset of a person who is thinking about being an owner. Because a true owner is a good leader, and good leaders lead from the front but put themselves last.

Being an owner is a lifestyle more than a career. By this I mean you really don't disconnect from your business; it's always there, 365 days a year. It's there doing what it does. The company doesn't stop when you take time off or get sick, have a family emergency, or just want some time to "chill out."

So, if you are the kind of person that needs to disconnect completely from your job in order to focus and enjoy your family, your hobbies, and your vacations, then I would advise against owning a service company. It will devour you, as this service company is composed of mostly people and not machines that you can turn on and off at specified times.

I've always enjoyed being available and solving problems both mechanically and logistically, whether over the phone or on the job. It's just part of my DNA. And I've been fortunate to have a wife who understands my passion and loves and supports me no end. And believe me, the freedom she gives me to be what and who I need to be, at generally the most inconvenient times, is incalculable.

For those aspiring to rise up through the ranks and into ownership someday, hopefully I've done a good job of portraying some of the realities involved.

I'll end this section by putting in my own two cents for those still contemplating their long game: Don't pick your career based on financial freedom alone. If you follow your passion, in time financial freedom will find you and you will enjoy the journey at the same time. This happens whether you decide to be an employee or employer.

People that are passionate about their jobs are always among the top achievers in whatever field they choose. I'm just a bit biased and want the trades to get their fair share of attention from the upcoming workforce.

IS THE JUICE WORTH THE SQUEEZE?

have a saying from the Dalai Lama on a plaque in my office. It says, "Judge your success by what you had to give up in order to get it."

I suppose hindsight is 20/20, but I have always tried to evaluate my work-life balance so I wouldn't look back and regret my decision to be in the service industry.

With that being said, I'll say there were many times when I pondered the thought of getting a 9-to-5 job so that I would have the ability to disconnect from my work. *Let it be someone else's problem for once,* I'd think. The idea of actually knowing what your paycheck was going to be week over week was an intriguing one. Planning a vacation and knowing that when it came you could just say, "See you in a couple of weeks!" and post-vacation just return to start back right where you left off! What a concept!

Working in the service industry is not for the faint of heart. Being the owner of a service company is even more challenging. You must become a master of both logistics and prioritization rather quickly to survive this journey in a professional manner.

Something my grandfather told me that I remember to this day was, "If you learn to keep your head on straight when all those around you have lost theirs, you will be a successful man or woman." And while it sounds like a paraphrase of a certain twentieth century poem (*If* by Rudyard Kipling), I have learned that this applies to modern life as well.

Taking my grandfather's words to heart, I did my best to keep my head on straight as an owner by making my work enjoyable. I also surrounded myself with like-minded people as much as possible. Over time I found that I was building a work-life balance that didn't require a vacation to merely recharge. I actually learned to rejuvenate my brain. I was never one to totally disconnect from my job and didn't feel the need to do so.

The lesson here is that life is short. Make the best of every day. Keep things simple and don't underestimate the power of a paradigm shift—it's not as difficult as it sounds.

After it's all said and done, I can now answer the question. Yes, the juice is most definitely worth the squeeze! I feel like I have received much more than I gave up.

I'll end this with two quotes I've always favored.

"A company absolutely devoted to service will have only one worry about profits. They will be embarrassingly large."—Henry Ford

"There are no traffic jams along the extra mile." —Roger Staubach

BREAK EVEN OR BUST

There are two little words that have a huge impact on the success of any plumbing service company

They are the lifeblood of all businesses in general. These two words are "break even."

For several years I ignored the term. But let's put a definition to the words break even. It's only possible for a company to pass the break-even point when the sales revenue and the cost of sales are equal.

Well, that's just common sense. Any idiot knows that. Indeed, so I thought until one day I met with my CPA to get my quarterly estimated tax coupons.

I said, "Sandy, this can't be correct, you must have me mixed up with another client."

She replied, "No, that's you! You had three really good quarters! Be thankful you must pay taxes. That means you are making money!"

"Well, maybe so," I said. "But not enough to cover my tax bill."

One thing led to another, and she asked to see my monthly profit and loss reports.

"My what?" I said.

She gave me a little smile and said, "You are kidding me, right?"

We had a "Come to Jesus" meeting and she gave me a homework assignment, which was to list all my expenses. Then we added to that the cost for payroll, which was an eye-opener. We put a chart together that showed what it cost per hour per employee with a new term referred to as "burden."

"What the heck is burden?" I asked. "If I pay someone $20 per hour, how can it actually cost me $33 per hour?"

I found out that workers' compensation and general liability insurance are based off of payroll. I had to pay half of each employees FICA and Medicare. I was paying 50% health insurance, short-term disability…. It went on and on.

To get to the short of it, we came up with my "break-even" number. What it actually costs to pay all my bills and have zero left in the bank account.

I could not believe my eyes.

Now I'd been in business for three years at this point and thought I was doing okay. But I was stealing from Peter to pay Paul.

My next challenge was figuring out how to raise my prices enough to break even and provide at least a 5% to 7% net profit.

Sandy told me, "You have the knowledge now. Go use it to run your business properly."

I found that knowledge is power, and it gave me the abilities necessary to do just that. I raised my prices immediately. And yes, I had pushback from some of my clients, but it really wasn't terrible. I soon had the financial resources to grow the company and never touched our line of credit again.

What a wonderful lesson learned before I went bust.

When you surround yourself with smart people, you can trust that things will happen a lot easier!

Now I joke around with everyone and say, "We've broke even and it's only 10 o'clock in the morning! Gonna be a good day!!" And I can actually believe myself!! Now that's powerful stuff.

Now I include this information in my Key Performance Indicators (KPIs).

As time went on, I met with a business coach that helped me put together a dashboard with my KPIs and a process to track important information on a weekly basis instead of a monthly basis. As well as to allow me to compare the same week, month, and quarters from the previous year.

In a short time, I went from not understanding break even to being able to determine my net profit on a weekly basis. Now that's called working "on your business."

I'm writing this not to toot my own horn but rather to provide the information necessary to not go bust. So many of us who are great with the tools of the trade create a business of our own only to find frustration and financial difficulties that take away from our dreams.

Being in the service industry and starting your own business is not for the faint of heart. But if you do, I hope my experiences save you some time, aggravation, and money. Cheers!

THE ONE-TRUCK EXERCISE

E arly on in my time as an owner of a small plumbing service company, I tried an experiment with a few of my service plumbers. I referred to it as the "One-Truck Exercise." I learned this from an industry-aligned organization I belonged to.

The purpose of this experiment was to give some understanding to my employees on two aspects of the business. Firstly: Where does the money (a lot of it) that comes into our company go. And secondly: To express the importance of being efficient and the true hidden costs of inefficiency.

First, I put together a basic list of expenses it takes to keep one service truck running for one year. After that, I met one on one with the service plumbers in my office. The list of expenses was on a large easel. I asked them individually to fill in what they felt was a fair dollar amount for each item for the entire year.

After each technician filled out their expense report, I would flip a page over on another easel that listed the actual costs.

We would review each item together to see how close we were.

Below, I have included the list along with a percentage or comment related to how close my service plumbers got to the actual costs. Let's take a look!

- **Truck payment.** We were within 5% of each other.
- **Auto insurance.** We were within 10% of each other.
- **General liability.** Not even close—they were an average of 40% lower.
- **Worker's comp.** Most just guessed but averaged 30% lower.
- **Health insurance.** Pretty close at 10% or lower, but the number was a wake-up call.
- **Fuel expenses.** This is just when a technician takes the truck home. We were 30% apart. (This was embarrassing—they were too used to swiping the company card. This showed how much of a benefit a company vehicle really is.)
- **Truck repairs.** Pretty close, as our fleet is rather new—within 10%.
- **Truck maintenance.** Within 10%.

- **Truck inventory.** Not even close.
- **Payroll.** This got complicated when I showed actual payroll taxes (half of FICA, Medicare, Simple IRA 3% match, health insurance, etc.). We were so far apart that I'll leave it at that.
- **Holiday pay.** Not close due to not understanding burden listed in payroll.
- **Customer chisel.** This is a term we use for the fact that some people will never be satisfied. Some guessed okay, but they were usually 50% too low (and couldn't believe we had to barter after the job was completed).
- **Warranty issues.** This was another eye-opener. Numbers were all over the place, but in general their estimates were 60% to 70% too low.
- **Call-back labor and materials.** Same as above. I actually had to pull out job-costing invoices to prove to a few that they did cost the company this amount. (Funny how we forget something like an actual call-back!)
- **Downtime for technicians.** This includes time in between calls, phone is slow or lacks connectivity, truck maintenance, and so on. They were an average of 40% lower. (A few had to see daily reports on themselves to believe the number. This is a report that

shows billable time versus payroll hours. Then transferred into an efficiency report per technician. This was truly an eye-opener for many when they saw their own efficiency reports.)

- **Advertising.** Not even close enough to mention.
- **Telephone.** Within 20%.
- **Office and inventory space rental fees.** Within 10%.
- **Office supplies.** Across the board, most were off by 25%.
- **Electronics.** This includes cell phone, iPad, office computer, and printer. Pretty close—within 5%.
- **Sick leave.** This includes lost productivity when technicians are absent. Not close enough to list but opened some good conversations.
- **Salary and benefits for office personnel.** The people who answer phones, book and dispatch calls. This was 30% too low.
- **Cost for payroll processing.** Most guessed at an amount per check and we were only $10 apart.
- **Cost of minor mishaps.** These are things that aren't turned in to our insurance like carpet cleaning, minor painting, drywall repairs, and the like. Holy moly! We were so far apart

again I had to pull vendor invoices showing what we paid out to correct those scratches to floors and walls and stains on carpets while carrying that old water heater up the stairs! (Yep, it happens even to the most cautious technicians!)

- **GPS and dash-cam services.** Calculating for just one truck. Most were pretty close actually and some were right on.

This exercise was mind-blowing for both parties. The actual numbers were eye-opening for the technician and it helped me understand why they felt like they could easily be paid more than they were earning. This exercise brought a new understanding to both me and my technicians. I saw a mindset change in several as their decision-making was influenced by the newfound knowledge of what it really costs to keep just one service truck on the road.

Another thing this exercise did was open a two-way conversation about some of the processes and procedures required in the business.

"It's necessary to measure efficiency and productivity on everything," I'd explain. "I know you hate these reports. But it is a necessary evil in all companies."

This exercise was a win-win. They got a small taste of what it takes to run a service business, and I had the opportunity to better explain why we do what we do, and that I'm not just randomly coming up with these SOPs and KPIs. And yes, the majority of Snider's Riders know what these acronyms stand for, and how they affect them.

Standard Operating Procedures and Key Performance Indicators will fade into the sunset if allowed, but they provide a foundation that is always there when a gentle reminder is in order. It also puts a very realistic understanding on what it costs the company to employ their services. It provides more information to the service plumber on whether to increase their skill set and stay with a good company that will be around for decades to come or put on their entrepreneurship hat.

Whether there's one truck or 15, the job of the owner is very different from that of a technician, manager, and even supervisor. As an owner I've taught this to several enthusiastic technicians over the years as they branched out on their own. Two of them still reach out to me from time to time. The conversation always starts with, "Hey, boss! How in the heck did you stay so calm?! You got a few minutes to talk?"

I'll end with two quotes, one from Peter Drucker that I tried to always live by. "You can't manage what you can't measure." And Stephen Covey says, "Seek first to understand before expecting to be understood."

And for the technicians, having your performance measured is necessary for the owner to run a well-oiled machine that will provide great customer service and a great place to work for decades to come. By better understanding your boss's job, you have a better understanding of what he or she needs from your piece of the puzzle. I can assure you that if you take a little time and apply these principles to your daily routine, you will be noticed faster than your peers.

ANOTHER KIND OF DASHBOARD!

As my bookkeeping and business management skills improved, I knew I was still missing a piece of the puzzle. I had a report on just about everything, but it felt like a false sense of security. It was at this particular time that I met a new business coach and we worked together to find my missing link.

It turns out that I had placed myself into information overload. That's when I learned that a dashboard is much more than the panel facing the driver or pilot with information related to the vehicle or plane they are operating.

When you're driving your car, you usually pay attention to things like the speedometer, fuel gauge, temperature gauge, and oil pressure gauge. As a business owner, I had access to the information related to all the moving parts of my plumbing company. But it was too much to keep track of all the time, and if I waited until a warning light came on, then it was too late and I was already in damage control instead of being proactive. That's where I was in my career as an owner. I was reading too many reports and not really able to decipher the information properly.

This is where I think I can save aspiring owners much time, heartache, and anxiety.

It didn't take my coach long to realize I was micromanaging my chart of accounts. He asked me to pick only five of the 15 Key Performance Indicators (KPIs) I was keeping track of on a weekly basis.

"That's impossible!" I said.

He pushed back and used the scenario of a pilot.

When a pilot is flying a plane, they have access to all information about the plane, but they mainly pay attention to just 4 or 5 gauges, such as altimeter, airspeed indicator, attitude indicator, heading indicator, and vertical speed indicator. The pilot monitors the most important functions of the plane. If one of them gets out of whack, then he or she goes deeper into the problem, but otherwise they know the crew members are doing their jobs correctly and keep their eyes straight ahead on the set destination.

"That's what *you* need to do," my coach told me. "So, pick your five gauges and let's create your dashboard."

I was able to whittle it down from 15 to 7 KPIs. We put an Excel spreadsheet together with our weekly goals for each KPI and a place below to insert the actual weekly numbers.

Oh my gosh, what a simple and beautiful concept!

For the first time in my career, I felt like I was actually driving the business instead of sitting in the back seat and just watching where we were going.

This dashboard serves as a set of headlights for my business vision. If a number gets out of whack, then I go find the problem right now. Not after I review a monthly P&L, or—even worse—a 13-week quarterly report.

I am now working in real time and hitting problems head-on while it's easier to find the root cause and make the necessary corrections.

Now we are measuring ourselves on a weekly and even a daily basis. And with this new foundation of information I can evaluate, not guess, whether or not we are on track to meet our projected goals. If we are, that's fabulous; if not, then we have time to make changes much earlier in the same quarter.

It didn't take me long to become very engaged in my new dashboard. In order for me to obtain accurate information, I gave each KPI an owner. That person was responsible for keeping track of that particular KPI. All seven reports were on my desk by 9:00 AM every Monday. Then I would plug the actual numbers into the spreadsheet, and it would generate a report telling me if we met our weekly goals. If we exceeded our set goals, I knew where we were excelling; if we were below our set goals, I knew where to go to get back on track.

I'll list my seven weekly KPIs below and then give a couple of examples of how it helped me run the company.

- **Weekly productivity.** (Total revenue broken down per technician.)
- **Weekly payroll expenses.**
- **Number of service-call runs.** (Also broken down per technician.)
- **Number of new clients.** (And how they found us.)
- **Number of water treatment installations.**
- **Number of "Happy Calls" made.** (Checking on clients a day or two after jobs to be sure they were completely satisfied.)
- **Number of estimates given.** (Also how many of those became signed and approved work orders.)

Here's an example of how this information was helpful in managing the team. Let's say we have a grumpy technician, and their call-back ratio is a bit high that week. Before I met with him or her, I would look up how many service calls were on their schedule and then explore the GPS history to see what time this individual was heading home. It was usually obvious that too many calls were put on this technician's schedule. So, before tempers flared and morale sunk any deeper, a conversation was initiated and a show of appreciation with an early out Friday. These swift actions helped to relieve the feelings of being unappreciated by the clients or the team, or worse, being hung out to dry when a client complained.

This application of the KPIs might sound simple, but when you as the owner get caught up in the everyday challenges, it's easy to take things for granted. Such as a good technician working too many late days in a row and beginning to approach burnout.

Another example of the usefulness of the KPIs is related to productivity. If I had a yearly goal to gross 1 million dollars, then I needed to produce $19,231 per week. Well, this dashboard took into account the roller coaster ride of survival in the service industry. I used to look at a monthly P&L.

Now I am analyzing our productivity weekly and able to realize that just because we're off 20%

this week, it's okay, as we were up 25% the week before. The ability to access the financial health of the company on a weekly basis is a huge factor in keeping a clear head and keeping my focus on the vision of the company.

This was one of the most eye-opening and morale-boosting things I ever put together. It helped everyone in the office to better understand each other's jobs as well as feel more a part of the company's overall goals. The goals felt more realistic, and as a result, there was less lamenting along the lines of, "Oh boy, the boss wants to do $2 mil this year!"

When I said it helped the inside office people better understand each other's jobs, it's real. Because they found out that in order to get necessary information for accurate numbers for their KPI, they had to get some of their information from a coworker. For the first couple of weeks, I heard around the office things like, "I didn't realize that you did that!"

A year later, we had a proven track record of our performance in these seven categories.

As we continue, we can compare our current numbers with those numbers from the previous year. Now that's a powerful tool! Talk about setting realistic goals and having a better understanding of how to get there.

The next year I played coach and went to everyone that had ownership of a KPI for the previous year and presented this challenge: "Now that you understand the concept and the importance of what you have done, please give me one or two ideas of how you can obtain the information you need to complete your KPI weekly report."

For example, the person in charge of the KPI for inbound and outbound calls was also responsible for tracking new clients as well as where they found out about us. So, this person actually created her own mini dashboard and shared it with those she learned were responsible for some of her needed information.

By the middle of our second year, using both micro and macro dashboards, we were becoming a well-oiled machine.

To end this section, let me say this: Pick the true performance matrixes that drive your business, then give ownership of that indicator to responsible people in that particular category. After that, simply keep them on track and you will be surprised at the load it takes off your shoulders. You'll be a more confident and optimistic leader. And because confidence and optimism are contagious, you and your team will be able to enjoy the journey more!

THE GOOD, THE BAD, THE UGLY, AND THE FUN

I've thought a lot about my position as CEO of a small and medium-sized plumbing company. My experiences and duties as owner might be classified as the good, the bad, the ugly, and the fun. I'll explain with examples.

THE GOOD.

I'll start with the definition of the good in this case: To be desired or approved of.

I learned early on that your circle of influence is a powerful thing. I've almost always been blessed to work with people who don't want to be average; they want to be special. They come in all types of personalities—extroverted, introverted, detail-oriented, risk-takers, visionary, and conscientious (to name just a few).

One of the best parts of my job was creating an environment in which these types of people could excel.

It was good to watch what happened when you actually got the right person into the right spot.

It was good to make job checks during an installation or repair and know that you would be greeted by a happy and satisfied client.

It was good to watch my coworkers come out of their shell and not be afraid of making a mistake.

It was good to watch technicians and inside staff go from being dependent on others to becoming independent and able to help their peers.

It was good to hear someone in the company protect the core values of being one of "Snider's Riders."

It was good to be called the Boss. You can own the company, but you're not the Boss until your teammates call you the Boss.

That's a whole lot of good stuff an owner can look forward to, but it doesn't come without some bad stuff mixed in.

THE BAD.

The definition of bad in this context: Having to deal with poor quality or low standards.

I have to start out with what might be a flaw in my personality. It has been said that I put my head in the sand. I avoid confrontation. Well, that's partially true, but I refer to it as my "rose-colored-glasses syndrome."

Before I'm too quick to put things into the "bad" category, I have to put on my rose-colored glasses. I take a good look from a different perspective. I try really hard to understand what happened and why it happened. When I take the glasses off, if I still see the same thing then, yes, it goes into the bad category, and I do what I have to do.

One downside of the position of owner was having to be the "bad guy" when it was necessary to protect the culture.

This normally took place when someone mistook my kindness for weakness.

Another bad part of my job was having to make the call when it was time to remove mercenaries from the teams.

Another bad part of this position is having to worry about the safety of your people during extreme weather conditions or late-night service calls. Even on a regular day, you worry about just getting everyone home at a decent hour. I know it's the nature of the beast and that's what we bosses have signed up for, but it's probably at the top of the "bad" list for this position.

THE UGLY.

I'll start with the definition of ugly in this context: Having to endure that which is unpleasant or repulsive.

I suppose both of these words could describe what a service plumber experiences on a normal basis but, as the CEO, that's not what I consider ugly.

To me, ugly is deception. By this I mean cheating, lying, stealing and just plain underhanded behavior. It's unfortunate, but there is ugly in the world we live in, and a good CEO will uncover and put a damper on such activities immediately.

THE FUN.

Last but not least is the fun part of my job.

The definition of fun in this context: The aspects of the work that bring enjoyment, pleasure, and amusement.

It's fun to be surrounded by good people. It makes being the Boss an easy job.

It's fun to watch our company grow and become a true brand of its own.

It's fun to finally be able to work *on* the company and be the vision guy.

It's fun to watch people grow and prosper.

It's fun to be a part of something bigger than ourselves.

It's fun to be of service to people.

It's fun to be able to solve problems, present solutions, and get paid for doing so!

It's been fun to have been both a plumber and an owner.

I'll close with this thought: When you like what you are doing—and are doing it for the right reasons—it's mostly fun!

FRONTLINE STORIES: OWNER'S MANUAL

THINNING THE HERD

Now here's a short story that I could write a book about, but I'll just say I almost let a few bad apples spoil the whole bunch.

Early in my entrepreneurial career I found myself in a quandary. I had not done a good job of putting the right people in the right places. Quite frankly, I had created a toxic workplace and was probably going to lose my best people and be left with all the underperformers.

The company, at the time, comprised 11 people counting myself. I made my first organizational chart on a piece of paper in about an hour. There were six names that were not in the chart. I couldn't find a place for them for one reason or another.

At this point, everyone drove their personal vehicle to the shop to start the workday. At 8:00 AM the day after my meeting with myself, I fired six people that didn't fit into the new org chart. I told the remaining five that if they decided to stay, I would always surround them with the best of the best. I apologized for putting us in a toxic environment and hoped they understood that I realized I had waited too long to make the terminations happen.

Almost immediately, the company became a fun place to work again, and the word synergy was an understatement.

It was that year that I hired another excellent service plumber, put him in my service truck, and got myself a car. I promoted one of my top guys to service manager and started acting like a leader. I actually used the org chart on that piece of paper to ensure I did not make the same mistake again.

LESSON LEARNED
Without good leadership, the inmates will run the asylum. You can create an interdependent workplace when you put the right people in the right places. This creates an environment that doesn't allow under-performing people to participate.

YOUR WORD AND A HANDSHAKE

Growing up, I learned that when you said you were going to be somewhere or do something, you did exactly that. And when you agreed on something, and shook hands, that was a binding contract. No paper and signatures were needed. This applied to banking as well.

So, it's 1985 and I needed two more service vans. I went to the bank and talked with John Palmer, the loan officer at Middleburg National Bank. I explained that the plumbing company was growing, and I needed to purchase two more vehicles.

He asked me a few questions and then said, "Go get your vans and bring me the purchase orders, I'll cut you a bank check to cover it and we'll set up your payment schedule later." We shook hands and off I went.

Yes, that's the way I borrowed money in the '80s and early '90s.

From time to time John would see me making a deposit and ask me to stop by his office for five minutes.

"How's business, Joey?" John would ask.

"Doing good, John," I'd respond.

John added, "Keep up the good work. Oh, and making those payments a week early doesn't go unnoticed. I'll be here when you need me again."

"Thanks, John, see you around," I'd say.

Those days are gone now, but at least I was privileged enough to actually participate in this type of financial dealing.

LESSON LEARNED

I have always tried hard to be like my banker, John. I understand that emails, text messages and Zoom calls are the norm, but I always dedicated a certain amount of my time to personally interacting with my clients, which included job checks and just a drop by to say hey. Those I didn't see in person received a handwritten note from me to say "thank you for your business" and ask how we are doing. (And yes, I sent these notes with a stamp on an envelope.)

THE COMPANY LOGO

As an entrepreneur, you are always looking for ways to make your company stand out and be noticed. At this point in time, I had several vans on the road, but they were not lettered or wrapped with our company name and logo.

With a very limited budget, I called a local company that installed vinyl signage on company vehicles. We worked together for a short time when I realized I'd bitten off more than I could chew for two reasons. First, it was going to cost a small fortune to hire a graphic designer. Second, I was still 80% in the field and 20% in the office. I didn't have time to dedicate to this project.

The owner of the sign company told me about an apprenticeship program at the local community college from which he had hired part-time interns. I contacted the professor of the graphic design department and in a short time he introduced me to two young students that needed to complete an outside project to complete their course requirements.

These two college students met with me multiple times. I gave them an idea of what I was looking for, and after several disappointing attempts on paper, they called me and said, "You are going to love this! We got your slogan ('If water runs through it, we do it') incorporated perfectly."

It was perfect, it was eye-catching, and the little relief valve shaped like a person blowing off steam just topped it off.

They put the program on a software disc that would download to the printer for my sign company, and we lettered and wrapped every vehicle in the company.

Now each van was a rolling billboard!! Our phones were lighting up like never before. I had people asking me, "How'd you get so big so fast?"

"How long have you guys been in Middleburg?"

"How many trucks are you running? I saw one of your trucks at my neighbor's house…."

It was as simple as letting people know who we are. We were the same company as we were three weeks earlier, but the new signage separated us enormously from our competition.

The owner of the sign company did me a huge favor by recommending the community college program, and he continued wrapping all of our vehicles until he retired.

LESSON LEARNED

Necessity is the mother of invention. Don't take no for an answer, just work from a different angle. Looking outside of the box is where many of the answers lie. If you want to be different from everyone else, you can't do what they are all doing.

I took this lesson and applied it to many more of our marketing strategies. I had always been unwilling to spend money on things where you can't always measure the ROI. But marketing dollars are, in my opinion, a necessary evil if you want to stay on top of the minds of your customers.

TEA AT 2:00 AM

My phone rang at 1:00 AM. "Hello?" I said, "Joey Snider here."

On the other end, a voice replied, "Joey, this is Diele. I have no heat."

It was January in Virginia. I asked if I could swing by first thing in a few hours.

"Well, it's very cold and my canaries and cockatiels probably won't survive" said Diele.

I replied, "I'll see you in 45 minutes."

When I arrived, I was faced with a Burnham V9 boiler with a cracked section that was spraying water into the fire box. There was nothing I could do tonight to repair the heating system.

Diele came down to the boiler room to discuss the problem and said, "Okay, you go out to the porch and get firewood and I'll make tea."

Long story short, we fired up six of the 11 fireplaces in the house. By 4:00 AM we had the main level at 70 degrees Fahrenheit. Her birds were happy. We had several cups of tea with cookies. I loaded up the fireplaces one more time so it would keep things warm until her staff arrived later in the morning.

We returned late in the morning to replace the boiler with a couple of modern high-efficiency boilers that actually hung on the wall and were back into service in another day.

Luckily, her fireplaces kept everything and everyone nice and warm until we were finished!

LESSON LEARNED

There are times when you just have to go above and beyond the call of duty! Personal relationships are crucial when running a service business. Long time and loyal customers need to be treated like royalty in the service industry. It won't kill you to go the extra mile when it's necessary.

WISHING WELL

If you have ever lived out of town, then you most likely will have your own water well. Inside the well is a pipe leading to the bottom with a pump attached. This pump works in conjunction with a pressure tank to provide constant water supply to your home. Well, when the pump down in your well fails, it needs to be pulled out and replaced.

This brings me to this story.

One cold winter day my colleague Mike and I were pulling up a well pump. We use a device called an Upsy Daisy. This machine attaches to the pipe going down into the well and we use it to pull 21-foot sections of pipe at a time until we reach the pump. This pump was hanging at 480 feet.

We were about halfway up when the portable generator cut off and the electric pump pulling machine shut down. We had just finished unscrewing the section of pipe and cut the wire when the wheels on the Upsy-Daisy started moving backwards. Well, the pipe slipped out of the pump jack and the remaining pipe, wire and pump went surging to the bottom of the well.

Mike looked at me and said, "Whiskey Tango Foxtrot!"

My heart was in my throat. This had never happened before. And of course, the customer just happened to be walking over to see our progress.

I could have crawled under a rock. But, like a true professional I said, "Everything is going well. It's a bit heavier than we thought so I'm calling a guy I know that has a crane truck."

The customer asks, "Is the quote you gave me still good?"

I reply, "Oh yes, still good."

I'm sweating bullets at this point; customer turns to go back to his house, and I call my buddy George. I get his answering service.

He calls me back in what seemed like hours (but it was actually only 10 minutes). I told him what happened, and he started laughing.

I was at my wit's end and he was still laughing.

I imagined the worst-case scenario—that we destroyed the well and a new well would have to be dug.

Finally, George says, "Calm down. Where are you and how deep is the well?" I told him and he said, "I can get it out for you—I'll be there in an hour."

When he arrived, we screwed on a fitting that looks just like a small cylinder-shaped toy called Chinese finger cuffs or finger trap. We fished around with this attachment hanging at some 250 feet down in the well, up and down and side to side for an hour.

George remarked, "It usually takes 25 minutes. Not sure what's going on!"

Finally there was tension on the cable. George hollered, "I got it!"

We pulled up the remaining pipe and wire, installed a new pump, pipe and wire, and just as the sun set, we were cleaned up and a happy customer was singing our praises.

LESSON LEARNED

If you pull enough well pumps, eventually you will lose one. At times it's not what you know, but who you know. This story is a perfect example of my 80/20 rule of life—that life is 20% what happened and 80% how you reacted. As an owner and a leader, you can't let anyone see you sweat!

WATCH OUT FOR THAT STEP!

Early in my apprenticeship working for my father, I was sent to install an outside hose faucet for a new client. I arrived and spoke with the customer.

"That's a great location for the new hose bibb," I told them. "I'll be done in an hour."

I measured and drilled my hole in the side of the stone foundation. I put the faucet into the hole. All that was left was to go into the crawl space and connect this to a cold-water pipe.

Off I went with my tools and torch. I spent 20 minutes looking for the end of the faucet and couldn't find it. I knew it was 30 inches to the right of the crawl space air vent. I measured it twice, but it wasn't there.

I came back out to measure again when it hit me! Oh no! There was a step down on the patio that I didn't account for.

I opened the door to the wood-paneled office and there, right behind the piano, was my pipe protruding through the wall. It barely missed the piano leg by half an inch. The hole I drilled was 12 inches too high, as I had not subtracted for the two steps.

My heart was in my stomach. I was devastated. What was I going to do? Surely my job was in jeopardy.

Well, I cleaned up my mess and showed my mistake to the housekeeper. She laughed and said, "Oh, Mr. DeButts is not going to be happy!"

I called the office only to get the answering machine.

Long story short, I drove back and explained what happened to my father. The look on Dad's face and the silence was more than I could take.

"What do we do?" I asked.

Dad called the client and asked when it would be convenient to meet on site and discuss the mistake and solution.

The next day at 8:00 AM we were in front of both Mr. and Mrs. DeButts. I was embarrassed and knew I had disappointed my father. I watched as my father explained how the problem happened, apologized for the inconvenience, took full ownership of the situation, and assured our clients that everything would be repaired properly and that the new hose faucet would be put in its proper location at no charge.

I watched as two very concerned and upset homeowners instantly became relaxed and very understanding.

Mrs. DeButts then put her arm on my shoulder and said, "I told Jon last night that your company would make this right. It's all okay."

This gets better. So, Mr. DeButts responded by asking, "Now that you are our plumber, could we solve the problem of the hole in the wall by installing a bar sink, cabinet, and ice machine in that area to cover up the pipe? And if so, when could we get started?"

My father later met with the owner's building contractor, and we installed the necessary plumbing for a beautiful bar in his office.

LESSON LEARNED

Take full ownership of your actions and don't be afraid of making mistakes. You can build trust and credibility under stressful situations. It's easy to be a superstar when everything goes perfect. But when a job goes south and you don't fall apart—that's when you become a true professional.

UNEXPECTED OPPORTUNITIES

This story took place around 1994. I had bought the adjacent building to expand our office and inventory space.

It was a Saturday morning, and I was busy building shelves when I got a tap on my shoulder. I spun around quite surprised to find my employee, Beck.

I said, "Hey, Beck, how's it going?! You scared the heck out of me!"

He said, "Sorry, Joey. I have something to talk to you about."

He put his Styrofoam coffee cup on my sawhorse and pulled up a bucket, so I knew it was serious.

Beck was my backhoe operator. I subcontracted him whenever I needed excavation work done. He was probably 72 years old at this time. He was a combat veteran in WWII and a medic in the Pacific Theater.

So, Beck says, "My backhoe and I are both getting too old, so I'm going to be your shop man. You got this new building and it's a mess. I'm going to get it organized and cleaned up for your guys. My pay is $11 per hour, and all I need is a coffee pot and rubber mats on the floor along the shelves. I'd like to start this Monday. What do you think?"

I was totally caught off guard. I started to laugh and redirect the conversation when that little voice started whispering in my ear: "Hey, knucklehead. Are you actually going to ignore the people who fought for the opportunities you are enjoying?"

After a moment's pause, I replied with enthusiasm, "Beck, this is perfect timing! I was going to run an ad in the paper soon. Monday is great!"

He smacked me on the back, picked up his cup and said, "I'll let you get back to it. See you Monday!"

As time went on, Beck did just what he'd promised. He even lined up the copper fittings in straight rows and dared anyone to mess with his inventory. If you put a straw broom away with the bristles on the floor, you were reprimanded: "Bristles up when you put it away; you can't sweep with a curved broom! You boys aren't wasting the boss's money on my time!"

Beck brought a much-needed sense of stability and purpose to the shop. The guys respected and eventually loved this tough ole bird. I learned a lot about life in the year and a half that Beck worked for me.

LESSON LEARNED

How easily we can let special opportunities slip past us if we deem simple gestures not worth our time.

Get as much knowledge as possible from anyone that is two generations older than you.

THIS THING CALLED CONTINUUM

I've been a member of several trade organizations. Some local, some nationwide. I've had six different business coaches. One thing about being an entrepreneur is that you have to know when to put your "rose-colored glasses" on and also when to take them off. I've always had a bad habit of chasing shiny things and went to many seminars, listened to audio tapes and CDs. I spent small fortunes on nationwide trade organizations. I knew there was a magic bullet out there and I had to be close to finding it.

It was 2015, and I was invited to attend a mastermind group on steroids called Continuum. I was hesitant as this group was just getting started and I was a battle-worn business owner who needed a higher level of camaraderie. Or so I thought...

I left the first meeting with a sense of curiosity. The second meeting I was intrigued, and by the third meeting I was enthralled and became a member.

A group of six to eight business owners quarantined together for four hours the third Thursday of every month. It turned out to be one of the best groups I've ever joined. I found a new way of dealing with being an owner/entrepreneur.

We all had different types of businesses, but the common denominator was the same. Second-guessing ourselves and lack of implementation. So off came the rose-colored glasses, and I participated in this group for three consecutive years.

LESSON LEARNED

Don't be mistaken, thinking that if you can talk the talk, you must be walking the walk. One invaluable habit I created by being a part of this group was that when I had an important decision to make, I would process all the information and make my own decision. Only then would I ask a respected handful of people for their opinions. If I was rendered an opinion that made me reconsider things, I would reevaluate my thoughts. But other than that, I didn't let others make up my mind and I stopped second-guessing myself.

This is probably one of the most valuable decision-making habits I've created or could pass on.

WE LOVE OUR PROPERTY MANAGERS!

All plumbing service companies love to develop relationships with good property management companies.

Once you have managed to prove that you are trustworthy to an organized property manager, you can then regard them as "golden eggs." And you take excellent care of them.

We had several of these property managers in our Rolodex, but one in particular stands out. Whenever she called in for service, the technicians would always vie to be the one to take care of her plumbing issues.

Well, one day she called in to complain about her dissatisfaction with one of my plumbers.

"I need to speak with the owner," she said to one of our office personnel, "and this needs to be resolved today!"

The message was relayed to me and an appointment set for that afternoon.

Well, I knocked on her office door. She said, "Come in and have a seat. I'll be with you in just a moment."

I sat in a chair just inside of her office and realized why the guys always wanted to be picked to run her calls—she was beautiful!

After she finished her phone call, I introduced myself.

She replied, "I'm Kristi. Thank you for coming to see me so quickly."

"My pleasure," I replied.

Some discussion ensued concerning her issues with our level of customer service or lack thereof. She made it very clear that she had always appreciated our high level of service, but the attitude of the plumber who came earlier in the day was not acceptable. We resolved the problem at hand, and I promised to be more hands-on with her account.

As time went on, I made a point of always returning the keys to her office. One day when I was bringing her keys back, I got up the nerve to ask her if I could buy her a quick lunch.

She hesitated but said, "Okay."

The rest is history, and I'll end by saying again, "Yes, I sure do love a great property manager!" We've been married for 16 years and are living our dreams together.

LESSON LEARNED

Don't hide behind an email or voicemail when you make a mistake. You just never know what the outcome might be when you take responsibility for your actions in person.

EPILOGUE

REDUCE YOUR LEARNING CURVE

A s I wrote this book, I asked myself a question: "Joey, if you were 25 years old and had a chance to do something different, would you do it again? If yes, what would you do differently, given the chance?"

With very little to no hesitation I know that I would still chase the same path. What a wonderful job and career I have had in the service industry.

Now for the second part of the question. There are a few things I'd like the chance to redo:

Number one. Realize that avoiding confrontation doesn't do us any favors.

Number two. Avoid writing position agreements or job descriptions around personalities.

Number three. Learn what the term "break even" really means. (What is the true cost of providing good, reliable service?)

Number four. Be okay with the fact that we can't be everyone's plumber. Know our customer, what their wants and needs are, and stay on track.

Number five. And finally, prioritize better communication with our client base. Be specific about what services we provide and how our operating procedures work.

I'll close with a final story regarding communication. As I mentioned briefly in an earlier part of the book, at one point I changed from time-and-materials billing after the work was completed to flat-rate, up-front pricing. Well, although this made perfect sense from a business perspective, my customer base threatened a coup d'état. I didn't know if the business would survive. The change caused a massive upheaval—pushback at every turn.

So I explained to my loyal customers that too many people were shocked at our invoices after the work was completed and that I had taken an average of 85% of the services we provided and put a flat-rate price book together.

Most told me, "Why in the heck didn't you write us a note and explain the change and why you made it? We get it and appreciate that your business model changes."

Wow, that was a lesson learned the hard way.

I've learned a lot from many wise people. I just wish I'd learned to listen more and talk less at a younger age. I'll end with three heartfelt quotes from three different clients that had been around the block and saw that I was giving it all I had.

Dick told me, "Joey, there ain't no goddamn dress rehearsal in this life we live. Stop second-guessing yourself and get on with it!"

Ed told me, "Joey, a fish rots from the head down, you know what I mean?"

Chuck said, "You've got to learn to trust—but verify!" (Obviously words from someone he valued.)

I always took heed to any advice I was privileged to receive from those with true empathy and wisdom. I learned a valuable lesson as I got older: Know the difference between unsolicited advice and true wisdom.

You will easily see the difference between these two when you first make up your own mind before asking for anyone's opinion. People with true wisdom are stingy in sharing their experience and knowledge with folks who talk twice as much as they listen.

I could have saved a few years of frustration if I could hit rewind and acquired these attributes sooner, but rewind isn't an option, and perhaps someone reading this might shave a few years off the learning curve if they can learn from my mistakes.

One of the beautiful things about gaining experience is that you can look back and see that most regrets were able to be overcome with persistence and a determination to avoid making the same mistake twice.

I hope my story will inspire someone to endure the ups and downs of a career in the service industry.

The sky is the limit, and the whole world is at your fingertips.

ACKNOWLEDGEMENTS

This book would not be possible without the steadfast support and love from my mother and father. Despite being one of five, I always felt like number one. That, in and of itself, helped us all to grow up to be the best we can be.

I owe a special thank you to my wife Kristi for her patience, understanding, support and unconditional love. She's a warrior and a treasure for which I'm grateful.

Thank you goes to Dennis and Jean Taylor of Paradigm Solutions for helping me with not only the title but putting my thoughts in a proper format for editing.

I'd like to thank Marty Paradise for his passion and dedication to being the best business coach I ever met. His ability to adapt and challenge his clients is priceless.

A heartfelt thank you goes out to all my lifelong and loyal clients that I had the privilege to serve. Earning your business and trust will always be a part of my life. I have had the privilege of working with and for so many extraordinary people throughout my career.

I owe a special thank you to all of my employees. They gave me the privilege and honor to be called "the Boss." Without their dedication and intestinal fortitude, I could not have made almost every client feel like they were the only customer we had that day. We weren't perfect, but pretty damn close.

TO THE VILLAGE OF MIDDLEBURG

Finally, a very special thanks to the village of Middleburg.

An hour west of Washington, D.C., my father started his first plumbing shop in the village in

1970 and I continued in the same location until 2021. The town of Middleburg was my home base for 38 years.

The loyalty, support and patronage I received from Middleburg, the local businesses, residents and surrounding areas is near and dear to my heart. It may sound cliché, but it was like working in Mayberry—that idyllic fictitious town of TV fame.

Working in a small community can be challenging, especially in the service industry, as everyone knows everyone else's business. But there's one thing that separates Middleburg and surrounding towns from many other places. The words tight-knit describe how people are in this little piece of heaven where western Loudoun and northern Fauquier counties come together. I had the privilege to be able to grow a plumbing and water treatment company in the midst of probably one of the most beautiful, peaceful and stress-free places on Earth.

Life is good, and I will always appreciate the village of Middleburg.

ABOUT THE AUTHOR

Joey Snider was the President and CEO at J. R. Snider Ltd. from 1983 to 2022.

He is a master plumber, gas fitter and water well provider. As for septic systems, he is a master conventional systems installer as well as certified to repair, maintain and install alternative systems in the state of Virginia, holding the AOSS licensure.

He is certified through VA DPOR as a backflow prevention device technical worker.

Joey is well known for his passion in the water treatment industry.

His commitment to the customer experience has made the brand J. R. Snider a household name.

The phrase, "If water runs through it, we do it," is synonymous with J. R. Snider.

Joey enjoys archery, hunting, fly-fishing and horseback riding with his wife and dogs.

With 46 years in the plumbing trade, Joey has been right in the mix of the plumbing revolution. He's a true professional and qualified to speak on matters of both technological and technician advancements.

Joey Snider